STORY OF
ELVIS

STORY OF
ELVIS

THE RISE AND FALL OF
THE UNDISPUTED KING OF ROCK 'N' ROLL

EDITED BY DAN PEEL

FOX CHAPEL
PUBLISHING

Used under license. All rights reserved. This version published by Fox Chapel Publishing Company, Inc., 903 Square Street, Mount Joy, PA 17552.

For more information about the Future plc group, go to **http://www.futureplc.com**.

ISBN 978-1-4971-0467-9

Library of Congress Control Number: 2024931807

To learn more about the other great books from Fox Chapel Publishing, or to find a retailer near you, call toll-free 800-457-9112 or visit us at *www.FoxChapelPublishing.com*.

We are always looking for talented authors. To submit an idea, please send a brief inquiry to acquisitions@foxchapelpublishing.com.

Printed in China
First printing

LADIES & GENTLEMEN

presenting...

The One and Only,
The King of Rock 'n' Roll
Elvis Presley

Nearly five decades after the premature death of Elvis Presley, still the biggest-selling musical artist in history according to several metrics, millions of us are still fascinated by him. Why is this?

Well, consider this. Elvis was born in an environment of extreme poverty that would seem completely alien to most of us today. With zero privilege and only his natural talent to sustain him, he rose to the status of global superstar by his mid-twenties, when the world lay at his feet. What could possibly go wrong?

Only everything, it turned out. Dogged by a laughably bad film career, emasculated by national service in the US Army and unlucky in love, Elvis found himself on a destructive path that ultimately led to his self-destruction at the age of only 42. Along the way, he morphed from the ultimate rockabilly bad boy into a harmless family favorite, and finally into a doomed shadow of his glorious former self.

This is why we love reading about Elvis, as you're about to do in this new and essential analysis of his life. How and why did he throw it all away? The lessons here are that talent and charisma will take you a long way, but too much money and existential futility will take you all the way back again . . . all the way to the end of Lonely Street, in fact.

Enjoy the story of Elvis. There will never be another musician like him. Celebrate his life with us.

CONTENTS

CHAPTER 1
ELVIS *Arrives*

CHAPTER 2
ROCK 'n' ROLL *Royalty*

CHAPTER 1

ELVIS Arrives

DISCOGRAPHY

The KING is BORN

We take a look at the early life and times of the man who would be known as "the king"—and explore where the seeds of his genius came from.

The story of Elvis Presley is one of a struggle against the odds that led both to success or to failure, depending on your perspective. In commercial terms, he has been equaled by a mere handful of performers since his death in 1977; in critical and cultural terms, however, it's arguable that he has never been surpassed, and never will be—the shadow he casts over the modern world is just too large.

What we can attempt to do, so long after his early departure, is figure out the truth behind the Elvis myth. Some elements of the tale are dramatic; some are comedic; others are most definitely tragic—and parts of it are far from true.

One of the key elements of the Elvis myth that is definitely correct, and historically provable, is that his rise to superstardom was rooted in a background of extreme poverty. His father, Vernon, a truck driver, and his

mother Gladys, a sewing machine operator, lived in East Tupelo, Mississippi, and were rocked by a series of catastrophes in Elvis' early life, starting with the stillbirth of his older twin, named Jesse Garon Presley. The babies were born on January 8, 1935, in a shotgun house—a type of wooden building that gets its name from the idea that a shotgun blast would pass cleanly from front to back. This building was constructed by Vernon specifically for the purposes of the twins' birth.

Vernon was asked about the tragedy in 1978 by *Good Housekeeping* magazine, and told his interviewer: "At that time there was almost nobody poorer than my wife Gladys and me, but we were thrilled and excited when we learned that we were going to be parents. I was only 18 years old, but throughout Gladys' pregnancy, it never occurred to me that I wouldn't be able to take care of her and the baby."

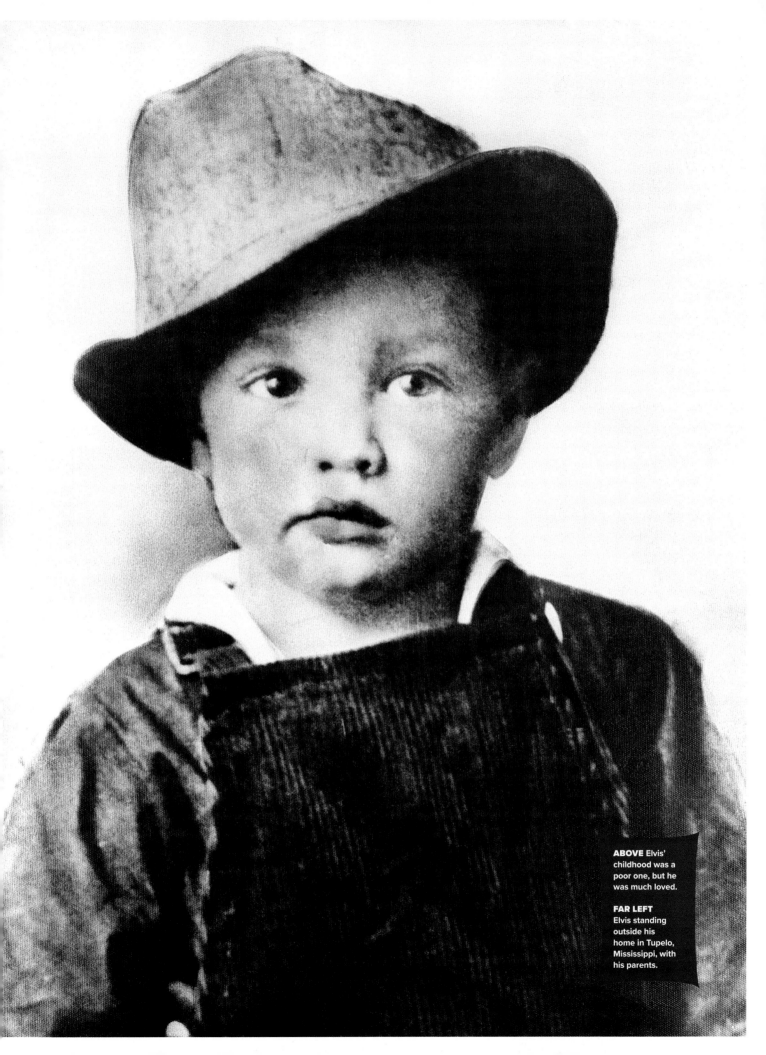

"I'VE NEVER HAD A SINGING LESSON IN MY LIFE . . . I JUST STARTED SINGING WHEN I WAS A LITTLE KID . . . I'VE BEEN DOING IT EVER SINCE.

★ *Elvis Presley*

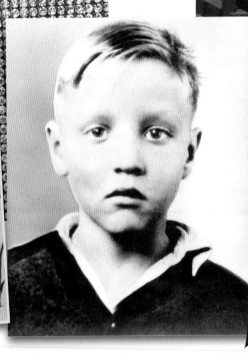

FAR LEFT A family portrait of Vernon, Gladys, and a very young Elvis Presley.

LEFT Elvis had a difficult childhood—his father was sent to jail, his family was extremely poor, and he was a loner at school.

He continued: "My parents were at our house with us, along with two women, one a midwife, who told us when it was time to call the doctor. After what seemed to me an eternity, a baby boy was born—dead. I was desolate at the loss of our child. But then my father put his hand on my wife's stomach and announced, 'Vernon, there's another baby here.' At the time Elvis was born, medicine hadn't advanced far enough for a doctor to predict twins, so his arrival took us completely by surprise. Our little boys looked something alike, but I don't think they were identical twins. Even though the elder one was dead, we named him Jesse for my father; the younger one we called Elvis, for me,

since Elvis is my middle name. We chose the middle names of Garon for Jesse and Aaron for Elvis, because we knew a couple whose twin sons had those names."

Never in permanent employment, Vernon moved from job to job several times during his son's early life. Although he had no previous history as a criminal, he served eight months for forgery in the notorious Parchman Penitentiary when Elvis was only three years old, during which time his wife Gladys lost the family home and the Presleys lived with their in-laws. Events such as this, and the poverty that plagued the family, made Elvis something of a loner after he started school at the age of six.

The boy's closest relationship was with his mother, and would remain so until her death in 1958. A 1981 biography of Elvis, written by the notorious Albert Goldman, implied the relationship was unnaturally close, to the point of making an impact on the young Presley's development; a more charitable conclusion expressed by Goldman is that Gladys possessed remarkable singing talent, so much so that she could reasonably be identified as the musical heart of the family rather than her son.

Despite this, music was not high on the agenda of the poverty-stricken Presley family, understandably enough. "I've never had a singing lesson in my life," Elvis told *Elvis*

BIRTHPLACE OF ELVIS PRESLEY

Elvis Aaron Presley was born Jan. 8, 1935, in this house, built by his father. Presley's career as a singer and entertainer redefined American popular music. He died Aug. 16, 1977, at Memphis, Tennessee

MISSISSIPPI DEPARTMENT OF ARCHIVES AND HISTORY 1977

Answers Back magazine in 1956. "No music lesson of any kind, in fact. I just started singing when I was a little kid . . . and I've been doing it ever since. I was 11 years old when I went in front of a real audience for the first time. It was at a fairground in the town I was born, Tupelo, Mississippi. I was shaking like a leaf, but I'd set my heart on singing, and nothing in this world could have stopped me from going ahead and entering the talent contest at the fair. I did it all on my own, and I didn't have any idea what I was going to do once I got out there in front of all those people. All I had in my head was the idea that I was going to sing."

He was referring here to an event in

MAIN Elvis' dad, Vernon, built a shotgun house when he discovered his wife was pregnant.

ABOVE The Presley's may not have known luxury, but they did the best with what they had.

ABOVE You can see the beginnings of Elvis' famous facial expressions in this photo of him as a child, posing as a cowboy.

BOTTOM Elvis in his high school ROTC uniform, taken 1955.

LEFT A bronze statue outside Elvis' birthplace house in Tupelo.

ABOVE A booth in a Tupelo restaurant where Elvis would go to eat.

1945, making him 10 rather than 11, as he remembered. On October 3 that year, Elvis entered and came fifth in a contest at the Mississippi-Alabama Fair and Dairy Show, where he sang Red Foley's "Old Shep," winning five dollars. "I didn't have any music or anything, and I couldn't get anybody to play for me and I couldn't play for myself because I didn't know how," he told *Elvis Answers Back.* "So I just went out there and started singing. I sang a song called 'Old Shep,' the story of a dog, and I know they must have felt sorry for me because they gave me fifth prize and everyone applauded real nice. Man, I'll tell you, I was really scared and shaking and all turning over inside. But I felt good, too. I'd been on a stage for the first time in my life."

The following year Elvis was given a guitar as a present and was taught the rudiments of how to play it by his uncle and a local pastor, although actual proficiency on the instrument always eluded him. At school, he began to absorb the blues and country music of the Deep South—and in particular Memphis, where the Presleys moved in 1948.

By his early teens, he had begun to affect an image which reflected his outsider status. Growing sideburns and sporting a ducktail and quiff—which led to minor blows with authority figures such as the school football team coach—Elvis spent much time listening to music in Memphis' African-American quarter, and in particular Beale Street, where blues and R&B were the standard fare.

"Later on, when I was 13 or so, me and a bunch of the kids would fool around singing," he said. "I never tried to go into any of the high school shows or anything like that, but I sure enjoyed beating up a storm with the other kids. And you know how it is. You get to trying different ways of using your voice and singing the words and such, and pretty soon you're singing in a style of your own." When he went on stage, he would take the guitar with him—not to play as such, but to use as a prop.

It wasn't easy going for the ambitious young singer, especially at school, where he underperformed academically. His schoolfriend and later bodyguard Red West told Todd Slaughter, president of the Elvis UK fan club: "[At school] we had crew cuts, wore T-shirts and blue jeans, Elvis had the long ducktail, the long sideburns, and he wore the loud clothes and naturally he was a target for all the bullies . . . one day luckily I walked into the boys' bathroom at Humes High School and three guys were going to cut his hair just, you know, to make themselves look big or make them feel big or whatever, and I intervened and stopped it, and I guess that stuck, because a couple of years later after Elvis had his first record, he came over and asked me if I would like to go with him, I think it was Grenada, Mississippi or somewhere, and I went and I was with him from then on, except for a couple of years in the Marine Corps."

In 1953, Elvis graduated from school and worked as a machinist and truck driver. As he told a press conference in Las Vegas in 1969, "When I was a boy, I always saw myself as a hero in comic books and in movies. I grew up believing this dream . . . When I got outta high school I was driving a truck. You know, I was just a poor boy from Memphis . . . I was driving a truck and training to be an electrician. I suppose I got wired the wrong way round somewhere along the line!"

It was around the same time that the Sun Records owner Sam Phillips was credited with saying that he was looking for "a White man with a negro sound and the negro feel"—because he thought that Black music such as blues would be popular among the White population if the right White artist could be found to sing it.

Coincidentally, Elvis recorded two demo acetates at Sun Studio in July that year, the first of which was a present for his mother. The songs were all popular ballads of the day and of little interest, but Phillips and assistant Marion Keisker liked the discs and asked Elvis to play with local musicians Scotty Moore and Bill Black.

Considering his options at that precise moment, the young singer could hardly have known how important this decision was. Can you imagine a world in which Elvis turned down the suggestion and walked away?

ABOVE After leaving high school, Elvis took work as a machinist and truck driver.

LEFT AND BELOW The blues and R&B music flowing from Beale Street had a lasting effect on a young Elvis.

Images Getty Images

" I ALWAYS SAW MYSELF AS A HERO IN COMIC BOOKS AND MOVIES. I GREW UP BELIEVING THIS DREAM.

★ *Elvis Presley*

ABOVE A high school performance by Elvis in 1955. Although he is holding a guitar, he couldn't really play it, using it more as a prop than an instrument.

ABOVE Elvis performs in front of his adoring fans in his hometown of Tupelo, Mississippi, in 1956.

BECOMING
The KING

Once Elvis' creativity was unleashed at Sun
Records, his first golden era began.

A s we now know, Elvis Presley made the right decision on that fateful day—and accepted Sun Records' Marion Keisker's suggestion that he come in and sing with the studio's in-house musicians. That decision meant a whole new period in American cultural history got underway on that day in Memphis, Tennessee.

As the well-known story goes, the historic moment for Elvis finally came one day during a break in Sam Phillips' studio. The trio—the singer, guitarist Scotty Moore, and bassist Bill Black—had been jamming on standards on July 5, 1954, when they slipped into a fast, impromptu rendition of Arthur Crudup's "That's All Right Mama," which Sam heard and thought might add a new flavor to the music of the day. He duly released the song as a single—and watched in shock as it turned the local airwaves red-hot.

Much later, Elvis told a Las Vegas press conference: "One day, I went into a recording studio and made a record for a guy named Sam Phillips on Sun Records. He put the record out in about a week. I went back to driving a truck and just forgot about it. Man, that record came out and was real big in Memphis. They started playing it, and it got real big. Don't know why. The lyrics had no meaning. I was just this kid, who went awopah-awh-a-awh on record . . . Anyway, they put the record out and it got pretty big in the South. But I still had my job. I was driving a truck daytimes and working nightclubs at night."

Moore, whose guitar playing on "That's All Right Mama" and many other songs, was integral to the early Elvis sound and remained a celebrated figure all his life, telling Music City Recorders in 1973 of the song's origins: "Sam Phillips and I would meet every day, drinking coffee and kicking around ideas

TOP Performing on the Louisiana Hayride, along with Scotty Moore and Bill Black.

ABOVE LEFT A young Elvis from 1953/1954, before his life—and music— changed forever.

ABOVE RIGHT Elvis' first single, "That's All Right Mama," released on Sun Records

about where music was going and what we should look for. In our conversations he mentioned that a young fellow had been in some time prior to cut a record for his mother. And he said he had impressed him very much, and they had kept his name on file and said, 'Would you get him in and audition?'"

He continued: "So Elvis came over . . . he had all the pink shirt, pink pants with the typical ducktail hairstyle at the time, white shoes . . . he was a little ahead of his time for the way he was dressed, which didn't bother me one way or the other, because I was interested in what he sounded like singing. We sat around for a couple of hours and he sang several different songs. At that time Bill Black lived just a few doors down from me on the same street, and he came over and listened for a while, and Elvis left and I asked Bill, 'Well, what do you think?' He said, 'Well, he sings good, he didn't really knock me out, you know?' . . . So I called Sam and told him basically the same thing—the boy sings fine, and in my opinion it would only be a matter of finding the right song and as to what direction, how he was recorded."

Images Getty Images

TOP Sam Phillips of Sun Records with the band.

LEFT The infamous Sun Studio, where it all began.

> ## " THE AUDITION TURNED INTO THE ACTUAL FIRST SESSION AND OUT OF THAT CAME 'THAT'S ALL RIGHT MAMA.'

★ *Scotty Moore*

ABOVE Elvis holds a stack of 45s of his single, "That's All Right Mama."

RIGHT As was common for the time, Elvis' early songs were covers.

Moore recalled the songs that Elvis had come up with: "He sang some Marty Robbins songs, some Hank Snow songs, some Roy Hamilton, some of the current R&B hits at the time . . . a little bit of everything, really. So Sam then did call him and set a time for us to go into the studio the following night. It was just me and Bill [as] a background, just to give us an idea of how he would sound like on tape. Well, the rest, of course, is history. The audition turned into the actual first session and out of that came "That's All Right Mama." We went in and went through several different songs and nothing was really happening, because you know it was an audition, and then we were taking a break, sitting around drinking

LEFT Elvis and Bill Haley on location for a short film in 1955. The film was never released.

MIDDLE Taking time out to attend the junior prom of girlfriend Dixie Locke, May 6, 1955.

RIGHT A classic portrait capturing the good looks of a young Elvis, taken in 1954.

coffee. Elvis started clowning around, he picked up his guitar and started dancing around and started singing "That's All Right Mama," and Bill picked up his bass, started slapping it, just more or less clowning, and I joined in and that's it . . . really, it's just one of those things."

The influence of this new sound on the musicians of the day was profound and immediate. As country star Waylon Jennings later wrote, "What if—I asked my dad one day in the early fifties—they mixed Black music with White music? Country music and blues? 'That might be something,' Daddy replied. On a fall morning in 1954, listening to KVOW's Hillbilly Hit Parade, I heard that something. I was taking my brother to school. It was about 8:20, and the reason I remember is that the program was only on for 15 minutes each day, from 8:15 to 8:30 a.m. Elvis was singing 'That's All Right Mama' and 'Blue Moon of Kentucky.' The sound went straight up your spine. The way he sang, the singer sounded Black. Maybe it was the flapping of the big doghouse bass, all wood thump, and the slapback echo of the guitars wailin' and frailin' away. It just climbed right through you. I had grown up hearing Bill Monroe sing 'Blue Moon of Kentucky,' but this was something entirely different. I thought, what a wild, strange sound."

None other than Johnny Cash explained the context of this new sound in his book *Cash: The Autobiography*: "There were a lot of White people listening to 'race music' behind closed doors. Of course, some of them (some of us)

were quite open about it, most famously Elvis. Elvis was already making noise in Memphis when I got there in 1954. Sam Phillips had released his first single, 'That's All Right Mama," with "Blue Moon of Kentucky" on the B-side, and it was tearing up the airwaves. The first time I saw Elvis, singing from a flatbed truck at a Katz drugstore opening on Lamar Avenue, two or three hundred people, mostly

teenage girls, had come out to see him. With just one single to his credit, he sang those two songs over and over. That's the first time I met him . . . I went up to him after the show, and he invited us to his next date at the Eagle's Nest, a club promoted by Sleepy-Eyed John, the disc jockey who'd taken his name from the Merle Travis song, and was just as important as [the radio DJ, no relation to Sam] Dewey Phillips

ABOVE Scotty Moore, Elvis, and Bill Black, set to change the world of music forever.

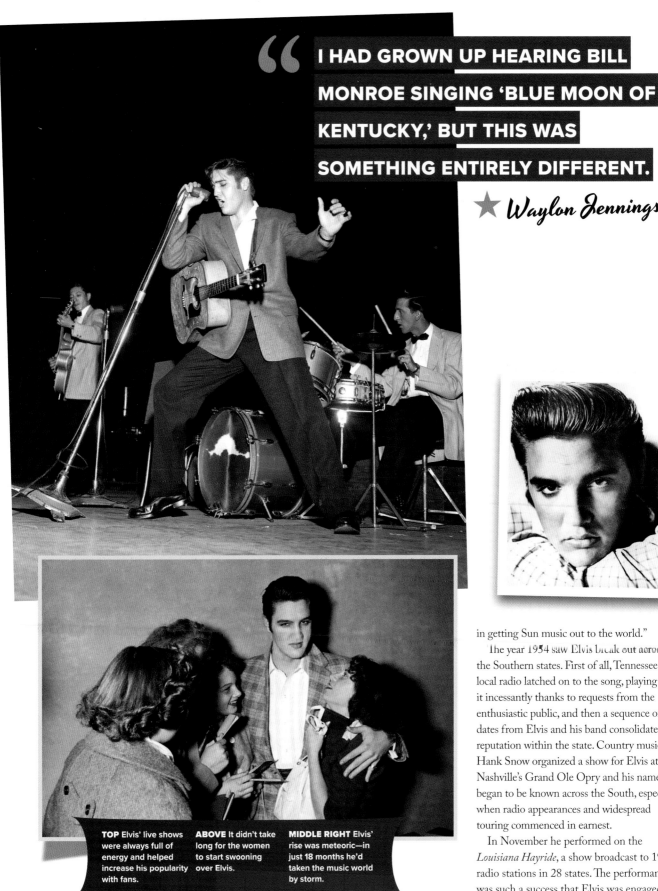

> **I HAD GROWN UP HEARING BILL MONROE SINGING 'BLUE MOON OF KENTUCKY,' BUT THIS WAS SOMETHING ENTIRELY DIFFERENT.**
>
> ★ *Waylon Jennings*

TOP Elvis' live shows were always full of energy and helped increase his popularity with fans.

ABOVE It didn't take long for the women to start swooning over Elvis.

MIDDLE RIGHT Elvis' rise was meteoric—in just 18 months he'd taken the music world by storm.

in getting Sun music out to the world."

The year 1954 saw Elvis break out across the Southern states. First of all, Tennessee local radio latched on to the song, playing it incessantly thanks to requests from the enthusiastic public, and then a sequence of live dates from Elvis and his band consolidated his reputation within the state. Country musician Hank Snow organized a show for Elvis at Nashville's Grand Ole Opry and his name began to be known across the South, especially when radio appearances and widespread touring commenced in earnest.

In November he performed on the *Louisiana Hayride*, a show broadcast to 198 radio stations in 28 states. The performance was such a success that Elvis was engaged to

ABOVE Elvis posing for a photo with his manager, Colonel Tom.

RIGHT Although his playing wasn't great, Elvis often had a guitar.

appear for a year of weekend shows, and a local DJ named Bob Neal became the trio's manager. A promoter named Colonel Tom Parker—neither his real name nor rank, as we'll see—was introduced to Elvis through Neal, and booked him to support Snow on tour in February 1955.

Things moved fast, with Sun Records releasing a sequence of singles by Elvis, Moore, and Black by the summer of 1955, with the band soon joined by a drummer, DJ Fontana. The "Sun years," as Elvis aficionados call this short period, must have been a rollercoaster ride from within, given the excitement of the songs—all cover versions, as was the standard for the era, but also a recurring practice through Elvis' career.

Collectors of mid-fifties rock 'n' roll will talk with baited breath of owning a complete run of Elvis Sun singles in mint condition, including Rodgers & Hart's "Blue Moon," "I Don't Care

if the Sun Don't Shine," made famous by Rat Pack crooner Dean Martin, the legendary "Good Rockin' Tonight" by Roy Brown, "Baby Let's Play House" by Arthur Gunter, Ray Charles's immortal "I Got a Woman," and "I'm Left, You're Right, She's Gone" by Kesler & Taylor. Listen to any of these songs and you'll be transported to a long-gone world: one where white jumpsuits in Las Vegas were completely unthinkable. These songs are the sound of a very young man blessed with boundless energy, nascent talent, and a big dream.

Colonel Tom, knowing full well what an opportunity he had, moved into a position of control over Elvis as the year passed, quickly securing him a record deal at RCA Records for the then-unprecedented sum of $40,000. Six months later, Neal was history—and the most significant commercial relationship of Elvis' career, with Parker, was cemented.

So how do we explain the speed of Elvis' early success, which essentially took place within a year and a half? Was it the fast, exciting music? Was it Elvis' remarkable looks? It was those and more, including his stage act—which, as we're about to discover, sent girls into a frenzy, and the authorities into an apoplexy.

Images Getty Images

25

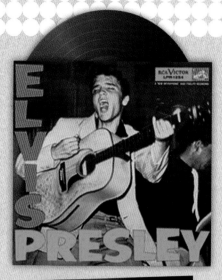

ELVIS PRESLEY

Released March 1956

As first steps into the public arena go, an LP that tops the charts for 10 weeks is a decisive opening move.

LEFT Elvis busy at work recording music in the studio.

ABOVE Setting some hearts fluttering with a few moves.

RIGHT Elvis singing to a hound dog, as you do!

There is no cooler shot of our hero than the dynamic image of the young blues-wailer that appears on the cover of *Elvis Presley*, confusingly the first of two self-titled albums released by RCA in 1956. To add to the confusion, there's a British version of the record, retitled *Elvis Presley Rock 'n' Roll* by its label HMV and featuring a different tracklist.

Still, there's nothing confusing about the astounding music captured in the grooves by Sun Studios' Sam Phillips and Stephen Sholes at RCA. It's as stripped down and raw as Elvis ever got, with the songs chosen to exploit the power of his still-untrained voice: listen how he roars through Carl Perkins' "Blue Suede Shoes" and "Tutti Frutti" by Little Richard, the latter perhaps the fifties' ultimate workout for any voicebox.

The *Elvis Presley* album was a commercial hit, spending 10 weeks at the top of the *Billboard* chart—the first rock 'n' roll LP to manage such a feat, and the first to make over a million dollars (worth more than 10 times that sum now). It introduced its star to a mass audience for the first time, although it's interesting to note that at this stage, the 21-year-old singer was just one of many contenders in the field. The album is best viewed from today's point of view as an introductory salvo, rather like the early records by The Beatles—still Elvis' only real competitors—when they came out seven years later.

Take the opportunity to gaze upon the face of the kid on the cover. He has no money. All he really has is a hefty dose of talent, the face and voice of an angel, and the desire to get those assets to the public as quickly and as convincingly as possible. Elvis would never be this innocent again.

TRACKLIST

SIDE ONE
1 Blue Suede Shoes
2 I'm Counting on You
3 I Got a Woman
4 One Sided Love Affair
5 I Love You Because
6 Just Because

SIDE TWO
1 Tutti Frutti
2 Tryin' to Get to You
3 I'm Gonna Sit Right Down and Cry (Over You)
4 I'll Never Let You Go (Little Darlin')
5 Blue Moon
6 Money Honey

ELVIS

Released **October 1956**

Hit 'em once, hit 'em twice—Elvis' second album of 1956 pulled no punches.

LEFT Elvis on tour with the Blue Moon Boys in 1956.

ABOVE Jerry Lee Lewis, Carl Perkins, Elvis, and Johnny Cash.

RIGHT Elvis posing for a portrait with a guitar, 1956.

A touch more sophisticated than its predecessor, the *Elvis* album—yes,isn't that title confusing?—offered his fans several pointers about where he was headed, creatively speaking. Firstly, RCA's Steve Sholes, who had co-produced the first Elvis album with Sam Phillips of Sun Studios, was at the helm for the entirety of the LP, delivering a big-budget, full-frequency production that replaced the tinny tones of yore with a luxurious sheen. Next, Elvis was a little subtler in his song choices, covering a ballad—the famous "Old Shep" by Red Foley, that had won him a contest prize as a kid a decade before.

Make no mistake, though, our boy was still full of rock 'n' roll enthusiasm, choosing to shred his tonsils on three Little Richard songs. Check out his full-tilt version of "Long Tall Sally" for evidence of his vocal skill and performance energy, as well as a reminder of the huge impact

that Little Richard had on an entire generation of White rockers. Songwriters Aaron Schroeder and Ben Weisman—a composing duo often employed by Colonel Parker in years to come—gave "First in Line" to the album, marking the start of a long and profitable collaboration for all parties involved.

Followed by a sequence of EPs and hits compilations, this LP is the second and final Elvis album from his early burst of rock 'n' roll inspiration: after this point, he pursued more diverse directions. That's not to say he abandoned rock 'n' roll altogether—after all, "Jailhouse Rock" was just over the horizon—but if you prefer your Elvis untrained, untutored, and a little bit uncouth, this is where that particular train stops. From now on, Elvis was just as interested in movies and all-ages music as he was in tearing up the stage.

TRACKLIST

SIDE ONE
1 Rip It Up
2 Love Me
3 When My Blue Moon Turns to Gold Again
4 Long Tall Sally
5 First in Line
6 Paralyzed

SIDE TWO
1 So Glad You're Mine
2 Old Shep
3 Ready Teddy
4 Anyplace Is Paradise
5 How's the World Treating You?
6 How Do You Think I Feel?

ELVIS' CHRISTMAS ALBUM

Released October 1957

Yule love Elvis' first foray into seasonal tunes. Eggnog aloft!

LEFT Elvis at a hospital with an injured finger, along with fans!

MIDDLE Looking good while posing in his Yuletide colors.

BOTTOM Not the real Santa— Colonel Tom and Elvis on a card.

S witch off your critical faculties: this is not an LP that bears serious analysis. *Elvis' Christmas Album* is all about the young star shining on carols, Christmas pop songs, and the odd devotional with all the sentimentality he could bring. Now, you'll actually witness some suitably stellar vocals here, for instance on "Santa Claus Is Back in Town," a performance of monumental proportions. Elvis really lays down the blues, with his voice sounding almost like the rasp of sandpaper, while his take on Irving Berlin's "White Christmas" is warm and affectionate, rather like a brandy sipped in front of a roaring log fire.

Then there's "Blue Christmas"—gently picked guitar, angelic backing vocals, and a rich, low-register delivery from Elvis—and "Santa Bring My Baby Back (To Me)," which will get even the most geriatric listener jumping around. If you're into more traditional fare, Elvis gives a perfectly pitched performance on "O Little Town of Bethlehem." It has a peaceful, lullaby-like quality, featuring the organ of Dudley Brooks, which creates the perfect atmosphere for drifting off to sleep.

Honestly, only the most hardhearted listener would dislike this album. "Silent Night" may boast a vocal style that has been parodied a million times by karaoke singers, but you can't beat the sentiment—which manages, just about, to steer away from schmaltz. "I Believe" is a pretty straightforward, gospel-flavored take on the Frankie Laine pop spiritual, with the kind of affected vocal that PJ Proby would later build a career on. Here, Elvis the spiritualist is on inspirational form. What's more, "Take My Hand, Precious Lord" is a change in tempo from the earlier raucousness as a showcase for Elvis' sonorous vocal chords, backed by a fittingly reverential atmosphere.

TRACKLIST

SIDE ONE

1 Santa Claus Is Back in Town
2 White Christmas
3 Here Comes Santa Claus
4 I'll Be Home for Christmas
5 Blue Christmas
6 Santa Bring My Baby Back (To Me)

SIDE TWO

1 O Little Town of Bethlehem
2 Silent Night
3 (There'll Be) Peace in the Valley (For Me)
4 I Believe
5 Take My Hand, Precious Lord
6 It Is No Secret (What God Can Do)

ELVIS IS BACK!

Released **April 1960**

Home from the army, our boy was ready to rock . . . but would America take him seriously again?

With everything to prove, having spent two years polishing his boots and being politely virtuous with Priscilla, Elvis needed this LP to be a good one. Fortunately, it boasts a ton of high points, with "'Make Me Know It" a pounding, gospel-flavored rocker and one of the standout cuts. Then there's the excellent "Fever," a song forever synonymous with Peggy Lee, but this take comes close, as it provides the perfect vehicle for Elvis' deep vocal register—it's a majestic reading of the standard.

Don't look for much subtlety, though: rock 'n' roll still runs in Elvis' veins at this stage. As the title suggests, "'Dirty, Dirty Feeling" is a straight, Nashville-styled rock 'n' roller. If you wanted to chart an alternative history of Elvis—staying away from the obvious choices such as "Hound Dog"—then you could do worse than starting here. As for "It Feels So Right," with the lines, "Step in these arms / Where you belong / It feels so right, so right," Elvis poses the question, "How can it be wrong?" Maybe he was posing this particular question to all his fans.

It's not all gold, of course. The slightly odd "Girl Next Door Went A-Walking" is a bit of lightweight pop-rock 'n' roll with a "doo-wah" backing. Jaunty, bouncy, and upbeat, it's karaoke fodder. On "Like a Baby," Elvis is a lover who cries like an infant because he can't break free from a deceitful partner. Is that really what babies do? A bluesy saxophone part gives the song some sparkle, fortunately. Still, there's always "Reconsider Baby" on which he wails, "You said you once had loved me / But now I guess you've changed your mind," with gusto and aplomb.

As comeback albums go, this one manages to do the job—just keep a finger near the skip button.

TRACKLIST

SIDE ONE
1 Make Me Know It
2 Fever
3 The Girl of My Best Friend
4 I Will Be Home Again
5 Dirty, Dirty Feeling
6 Thrill of Your Love

SIDE TWO
1 Soldier Boy
2 Such a Night
3 It Feels So Right
4 Girl Next Door Went A-Walking
5 Like a Baby
6 Reconsider Baby

ABOVE A warm welcome awaited Elvis on his return.

ABOVE RIGHT Elvis showing off his acting sergeant stripes.

RIGHT When rock 'n' roll met the biggest crooner in town.

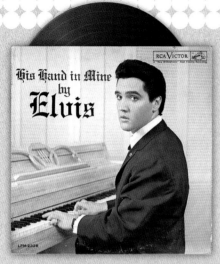

HIS HAND IN MINE

Released **November 1960**

When Elvis got religion, he got it good—here's his first big gospel moment.

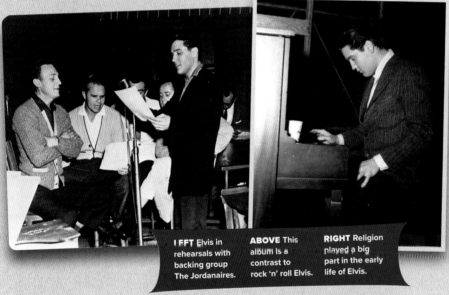

LEFT Elvis in rehearsals with backing group The Jordanaires.

ABOVE This album is a contrast to rock 'n' roll Elvis.

RIGHT Religion played a big part in the early life of Elvis.

Following up on the *Peace in the Valley* EP of 1957, Elvis went "full gospel" three years later with this devotional album, which will be of interest to readers of any or no religious conviction because it's so expertly crafted. It underperformed commercially compared to his earlier work, but that was only to be expected.

High points include powerful versions of "Swing Down Sweet Chariot" and "Mansion Over the Hilltop," while a take on The Trumpeteers' "Milky White Way" benefits from a bluesy delivery by Elvis, not generally known for singing in this style after 1957 or thereabouts. You can hear him dropping his vocal down almost to a whisper on the title cut, originally by The Statesmen, fully aware of the drama that is required to properly deliver the song.

Elvis' backing group, The Jordanaires, are featured at the beginning of "I Believe in the Man in the Sky," setting the scene before he enters with the big vocal guns. He's more subtle on "He Knows Just What I Need," though, with a keen awareness of the dynamics necessary to make this album appeal to his fans, even those of a secular persuasion. In some ways this is *His Hand In Mine*'s real triumph—as a showcase for its singer's awareness of how to make an unusual album sound like a great one.

It's interesting to speculate what *His Hand In Mine* really reveals about Elvis. He chose to return to the music of his childhood as early as 1960, perhaps bored by the raucous rock 'n' roll that he'd been singing for the previous five years. Maybe the sexual flavor of his performances had tired him out; possibly the real Elvis was a conservative, church-going type, not the boundary-breaking jailhouse punk, after all. These songs certainly portray him in a different light—but it's a convincing one.

TRACKLIST

SIDE ONE

1 His Hand in Mine
2 I'm Gonna Walk Dem Golden Stairs
3 In My Father's House
4 Milky White Way
5 Known Only to Him
6 I Believe in the Man in the Sky

SIDE TWO

1 Joshua Fit the Battle
2 Jesus Knows What I Need
3 Swing Down Sweet Chariot
4 Mansion Over the Hilltop
5 If We Never Meet Again
6 Working on the Building

SOMETHING FOR EVERYBODY

Released June 1961

Perhaps *Something For Some Of Us* would have been a better title?

LEFT A quick blast of drums while on the set of *Flaming Star*.

ABOVE Tackling questions at a press conference in Hawaii.

RIGHT Giving something for everyone while in Hawaii.

Recorded in just two sessions and split into a side of ballads and a side of rockers, *Something for Everybody* has a slightly overambitious title—as it's adequate rather than astounding. The ballads side is a touch sleepy, although "There's Always Me" reveals some nice vocal acrobatics from Elvis and "Gently" pulls the listener seductively inward. However, there's only so much smooth intoning a fan can take, and you can't help but yearn to flip the LP for faster material.

When this happens, it's very welcome. There's a real sense of Nashville energy about these latter tracks, aimed at male listeners because Elvis' female fans were thought to prefer love songs. This is nonsense, of course, and it's a safe bet that as many women as men who bought this record much preferred the uptempo tracks.

There's a lot of that to choose from, with "In Your Arms" and "Put the Blame On Me" giving us a welcome dose of the old Presley humor. A version of Bobby Darin's "I Want You With Me" is worth checking out, too, just to hear Elvis' take on the easy listening style. The other tunes, specifically "I Want You With Me" and "I Slipped, I Stumbled, I Fell," fly merrily by, and if there's nothing particularly persuasive about this album, it's at least moderately entertaining—on one side, anyway.

The main criticism that *Something for Everybody* faces is that the famous sense of dynamics that made the best Elvis albums soar isn't really there. The songs, perhaps because they were recorded in such a quick blast of creativity, suffer from a slight feeling of sameness, no matter how much vocal juice Elvis injects into them. Well, never mind—as mid-career Elvis releases go, this one does no harm. Just don't expect magic.

TRACKLIST

SIDE ONE

1 There's Always Me
2 Give Me the Right
3 It's a Sin
4 Sentimental Me
5 Starting Today
6 Gently

SIDE TWO

1 I'm Comin' Home
2 In Your Arms
3 Put the Blame On Me
4 Judy
5 I Want You With Me
6 I Slipped, I Stumbled, I Fell

ROCK 'n' ROLL Royalty

ABOVE In 1956, Elvis could seemingly do no wrong, often surrounded by adoring fans.

All HAIL The KING

The rise—and first fall—of the monarch of music: one of the great
rock 'n' roll sagas of our time.

I

magine the frenzy of activity in the RCA boardroom, back in November 1955. The suits at the record company had paid Sam Phillips the unprecedented sum of $40,000—worth more than 10 times that amount today—for a contract with his boy Elvis Presley, who, let us not forget, was still only 20 years old at the time. Just as dollar signs glinted in the eyes of the moneymakers over at RCA, they knew that they, and he, needed to work hard to recoup that enormous sum.

Colonel Tom, who is routinely portrayed decades since his death as a con man who ripped Elvis off and bled him dry, deserves at least some credit for making his protégé rich, even if his creative decisions on behalf of his client were questionable at best. He set up two publishing companies, Elvis Presley Music and Gladys Music, and even though Elvis never wrote a song of his own and used professional songwriters, the Colonel's infamous stipulation to these composers was that they give up one-third

or more of their royalties if they wanted Elvis to perform their material.

RCA knew, of course, that Elvis' reputation had been made on the back of raw, exciting rock 'n' roll, and promptly reissued a swathe of his Sun Studios material immediately after his signing. With the addition of a new song, the fabulous "Heartbreak Hotel," released as a single on January 27, 1956, Elvis now had a rich catalogue of current songs to play at the tours on which he embarked that year.

In this golden era—from '56 until he joined the army two years later—Elvis occupied a godlike position for millions of fans. His profile skyrocketed after three television performances on CBS's *Stage Show* in two months: since they were recorded in New York, Elvis seized the opportunity to record new songs, notably a version of Carl Perkins' "Blue Suede Shoes." Together with the release of the single "I Forgot to Remember to Forget," a previously released Sun recording, his self-titled debut album in March, and then two appearances

LEFT Elvis with Sam Phillips, Leo Soroka, and Robert Johnson at Sun Studio.

BELOW Television proved to be essential in growing the Elvis fan base.

BELOW RIGHT With host Milton Berle, after performing on his show.

BOTTOM Signing some autographs after appearing on The Ed Sullivan Show.

on NBC's *Milton Berle Show*, it meant that in early '56, he was inescapable.

Not that Elvis' teenage fans wanted to escape him. There had never been a star like him in music before. Frank Sinatra and Dean Martin, perhaps his nearest equivalents in stature, looked positively antiquated next to him. The mention of these two singers-turned-actors is relevant because, like them, Elvis wanted not just to be a musician but also a film star; indeed, it's been theorized that the movies was where his real ambition lay all along. By late 1956—a mere year or so into his first flush of fame—he had signed a seven-year deal with Paramount Pictures.

A show by Freddie Bell & The Bellboys in Las Vegas inspired Elvis to record a version of "Hound Dog," written in 1952 by songwriters Jerry Leiber and Mike Stoller. This song, an upbeat, catchy and—let's be honest—silly hit, became a Presley staple along with "Heartbreak Hotel," "Don't Be Cruel," and "Blue Suede Shoes" in this early part of his career, not least because he sang it

"IN THIS GOLDEN ERA—FROM '56 UNTIL HE JOINED THE ARMY TWO YEARS LATER—ELVIS OCCUPIED A GODLIKE POSITION FOR MILLIONS OF FANS.

Images Getty Images

37

to an actual dog on NBC's *Steve Allen Show*.

The summer of '56 was the Summer of Elvis. The "Don't Be Cruel" / "Hound Dog" single topped the charts for 11 weeks, and a September 9 appearance on CBS' *Ed Sullivan Show* pulled in an astounding 60 million viewers, over 82 percent of the viewing audience. Little wonder that none other than John Lennon, then a 16-year-old kid on the other side of the Atlantic, pondered a decade later that "Before Elvis, there was nothing."

The wisdom of this comment also lies in the fact that society was changing in tandem with Elvis. A new teenage demographic, equipped with hard cash for the first time, was the target of aggressive marketing by entities such as RCA, who had teen-friendly material ready to sell. Elvis, and his pelvic thrusts, happened to coincide with this cultural change, and even accelerated it to an extent. Parents watched this happen, with their reactions ranging from indifference to outrage, helping the

"AN APPEARANCE ON CBS' *ED SULLIVAN SHOW* PULLED IN AN ASTOUNDING 60 MILLION VIEWERS.

TOP Elvis recording at an RCA Victor studio in 1956—as his star was rising.

ABOVE Elvis was influenced by African-American stars like Mahalia Jackson (left).

RIGHT Having fun backstage with Liberace, both pretending to be each other.

Images Getty Images

LEFT Elvis showing his group a gold record for "Heartbreak Hotel," released in '56.

BELOW *Love Me Tender* may have been adored by fans, but critics hated it.

ELVIS PRESLEY

RICHARD EGAN · DEBRA PAGET
AND INTRODUCING
ELVIS PRESLEY
in
LOVE ME TENDER
A 20th CENTURY-FOX
CINEMASCOPE
PICTURE

DEAR MR. ROCK 'N' ROLL SING-
"LOVE ME TENDER"
"WE'RE GONNA MOVE"
"POOR BOY"
"LET ME"

...SINGIN' MAN
...FIGHTIN' MAN
...LOVIN' MAN

inter-generational schism grow faster and wider.

It's important to consider at this point, and throughout the Presley saga, the debt that Elvis owed to African-American music. Sam Phillips' famous maxim of a White man singing Black music being a recipe for success had come true to the extent of millions of dollars being earned and spent. Elvis' genuine love of gospel, combined with the rhythm and blues that had been invented by Black jazz and swing musicians as far back as the twenties, made for an irresistible mixture. His outrageous dance moves, shocking as they were to White TV-watchers, barely compared to those of many Black audiences, who had largely been forced to celebrate their music out of the public eye until then.

Not that much reflection on these lines took place at that point: in those early years, Elvis seemed utterly unstoppable. It's all the more disconcerting, then, when you realize how quickly he fell out of step with the changing times, left behind by the cool kids the moment he switched to recording ballads, acting in films, and losing his controversial edge.

You can arguably pinpoint this loss of momentum with the ballad "Love Me Tender" and the lackluster film of the same title, both of which made vast sums of money but were received negatively by critics, especially those who were fans of his earlier, rip-roaring music. Still, why would Elvis care? By the end of 1956 he was a pop star, a film star, and incredibly wealthy, having sold $22 million of merchandise— the Colonel's relentless genius at work there—on top of his massive record sales.

Before the end of the year, Elvis made history during a quick visit to Sun Records, where Carl Perkins and Jerry Lee

Lewis were recording at the time. Johnny Cash also showed up, and the four legends played a brief jam session together. Sam Phillips had no legal way of releasing the music they made, but the savvy studio owner made sure the session was recorded, although it wasn't released—officially, that is—for many years. Track the songs down: they're called the "Million Dollar Quartet" recordings for a reason, although "billion" might be a more appropriate word to use these days.

No wonder that by March 1957 Elvis was able to move into a mansion south of downtown Memphis called Graceland,

TOP LEFT Elvis bought Graceland with his newfound wealth in early 1957.

BELOW LEFT Getting ready for his performance on *The Milton Berle Show.*

BOTTOM LEFT Giving the audience exactly what they want in 1956.

ABOVE Elvis with Frank Sinatra, who had been very critical of rock 'n' roll.

Images Getty Images

bringing his parents with him. The property cost him around a million bucks in today's terms, and soon became a playboy's paradise staffed by a subservient retinue, the beginnings of the ever-present "Memphis Mafia" crew of trusted associates.

While he continued to top the charts with songs such as "Too Much," "All Shook Up," "(Let Me Be Your) Teddy Bear," and the *Loving You* soundtrack album, Elvis knew that his time as a hot young agitator was drawing to a close, as his mandatory national service was approaching. Classified 1-A and thus eligible for drafting into the army, Elvis was going to be a soldier.

Perhaps for this reason, 1957 was an incredibly busy year for Elvis, encouraged into activity by the intimidating Colonel. The "Jailhouse Rock" single, EP, and film was a better combined effort than some of his more recent music and acting, and three short tours kept his audiences happy. The cause was assisted nicely by Frank Sinatra, who whined that rock 'n' roll "smells phony and false. It is

sung, played, and written, for the most part, by cretinous goons." To his credit, Elvis shrugged this off with maturity beyond his years, saying "I admire the man. He has a right to say what he wants to say. He is a great success and a fine actor, but I think he shouldn't have said it . . . This is a trend, just the same as he faced when he started years ago."

Lightweight as the idea of a seasonal release might sound, at the end of '57 *Elvis' Christmas Album* was a huge hit, helped by a single called "Santa Claus is Back in Town." The LP sold a monstrous 20 million copies, and after a film role in *King Creole*—which was entertaining, in a tacky way—Elvis was drafted into the US Army on a wave of huge commercial, if not critical, success.

RCA had prepared for the absence of its cash cow from the public eye for two years by amassing a reserve of songs, scheduling them for release while he was away. Suffice to say that the public still loved Elvis, whether he was at home or on duty. While serving in the army he enjoyed 10 Top 40 hits in the USA: he also scored with four

albums, although these were compilations. After his honorable discharge at the rank of sergeant in March 1960, Elvis recorded a single, "Stuck on You," whose number one status seemed to indicate that he was still in favor with his fanbase.

Still, on returning to America as a civilian, Elvis clearly felt that he had ground to make up. Speaking from a press conference at his father Vernon Presley's office in Memphis a few days after he returned, he told the press about his plans for the year ahead.

"The first thing I have to do is cut some records," he explained, "and then I have the television show with Frank Sinatra, and then I have the picture with [producer Hal] Wallis, and after that, I have two [more films] for 20th Century Fox—and after that, heaven knows. I don't! I suppose that will keep me busy the rest of the year."

When one reporter asked a savvy question about whether Elvis thought that the popular music scene had changed while he was away in Germany, he paused to consider for a moment

LEFT Elvis taking a quick break from a hectic recording schedule.

ABOVE Captured before his show at the University of Dayton Fieldhouse, '56.

RIGHT After leaving active duty in 1960, Elvis became more mainstream.

FAR RIGHT Elvis made over 20 movies in the sixties—quantity over quality, alas.

before replying, "Possibly, yes. If it has changed, I would be foolish not to change with it, but as of now, I have no reason to change anything."

This was the right answer—both humble and guarded. Had pop music changed its spots between 1958 and 1960? Not drastically, no. Now, had the period in question been 1961 to 1963, when the world was rocked by the arrival of Beatlemania, the answer would have been quite different. Elvis was saved from utter irrelevance by a hair—a mere couple of years. Now, the task that lay before him was to regain his former status.

One thing to note is that now he'd served his country—and what's more,

> "ELVIS PLUNGED INTO HIS HOLLYWOOD CAREER, ALTHOUGH THIS PROVED NO MORE CRITICALLY SUCCESSFUL THAN HIS MUSIC.

TOP The face that launched a thousand ships—Elvis posing in his '56 heyday.

ABOVE In the studio recording another soundtrack for another movie.

got engaged along the way—Elvis could no longer be regarded a rebel by anyone's standards. Parents and grandparents liked the new, ballad-heavy approach that he took with his first post-army LP, *Elvis Is Back!*, and justifiably so as "It's Now or Never" and "Are You Lonesome Tonight?" were—and still are—great songs. However, Elvis could hardly perform those songs with the sexual fervor of 1956, making him a safe bet—a toothless hound dog, if you like. No wonder that another pithy John Lennon quote, "Elvis died the day he joined the army," comes to mind here.

His edge vanished completely when he played alongside his former nemesis Frank Sinatra on a TV show called

Welcome Home Elvis—earning $125,000 for eight minutes of singing—and recorded a gospel album, *His Hand in Mine*. By 1961, Elvis was all about making comfortable music, such as the country-style *Something For Everybody* LP of 1961, described by one critic as "a pleasant, unthreatening pastiche of the music that had once been Elvis' birthright."

Perhaps aware of this decline, Elvis plunged into his Hollywood career, although this proved to be no more critically successful than his music. He was still hitting the top of the charts with his albums and scoring big at the box office with his films, but by 1962 America was only a year or so away

from The Beatles-spearheaded British Invasion, and public tolerance for unchallenging art was on the wane.

Elvis made over 20 films in the sixties, but by the later years of the decade the idea of being a movie star had lost its appeal for him. He knew how creatively weak most of his movies were, but they made money, as did the accompanying soundtracks—according to Jerry Leiber, always made up of "three ballads, one

Images Getty Images, Alamy

ABOVE A candid moment capturing an exhausted Elvis on his knees after a show, with his friend offering a neck rub.

"
FACED WITH THE PROSPECT OF THE RECORD DEAL BEING PULLED FROM BENEATH THEM, COLONEL TOM DECIDED TO TAKE ACTION.

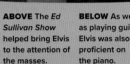

ABOVE The *Ed Sullivan Show* helped bring Elvis to the attention of the masses.

BELOW As well as playing guitar, Elvis was also proficient on the piano.

TOP Elvis in '68's Speedway as he focused increasingly on his movie career.

ABOVE By the end of the sixties, Elvis knew it was time to change or be left behind.

Images Getty Images, Alamy

medium-tempo number, one up-tempo, and one break blues boogie."

The films' decline in quality was not their only problem. This was the sixties, the most culturally progressive decade in history, and fans' tastes were changing quickly. Bubblegum music like the Elvis movie soundtracks was utterly disposable compared to new sounds from The Rolling Stones, The Kinks, The Who, Frank Zappa, Marvin Gaye, Sam Cooke, James Brown and, of course, Bob Dylan and The Beatles.

Popular music was now connected to protests connected to the civil rights struggle, the Vietnam War and anti-communist McCarthyism. Kids grew their hair and took drugs while the threat of nuclear war loomed. In that context, who gave a damn about Elvis—a hillbilly millionaire singing songs about partying on the beach?

To their credit, Elvis and Colonel Tom recognized that the rot was setting in and, although neither man was exactly what you'd call a visionary when it came to spotting social trends, knew that action needed to be taken if Elvis' career was to be resurrected, or even saved from disaster. From 1964 to 1968, Elvis only hit the Top 40 once, with "Crying in the Chapel" in '65, causing consternation at RCA. Faced with the prospect of the record deal being pulled from beneath them, Colonel Tom decided to take action.

Knowing that TV was where his boy would hit home best, Colonel Tom arranged for NBC to finance and broadcast a Christmas special in late 1968. How on earth this pitch must have sounded to the young executives at the network is not known: hip to the latest sounds from Deep Purple and Jimi Hendrix, they must have regarded Elvis as a dinosaur from a former epoch. Still, the deal was signed and a comeback show was scheduled.

It was the best decision that Colonel Tom, and by extension his famous client, ever made.

SYMBOL

The hottest thing on two legs since James Dean, Elvis thrilled America's youth—and terrified their parents

E lvis Presley was a beautiful man. It's not how we usually describe men, beauty being typically thought of as a feminine trait, and yet it's wholly appropriate in the case of the young Elvis, because his look was so bound up with femininity. He wore eye makeup; he had classic, rosebud lips; his hair was artfully coiffed. At the same time, he was undeniably male in his physique, his vocal style and his confrontational approach.

Most of us can handle this today, and thank heavens for that—but try and imagine the impact on the American public in 1957, when there was very little precedent for an entertainer who presented such a mixed message. Remember, Elvis grew up in America's Deep South, a poverty-stricken part of the world. Racism was rife; African Americans had been routinely lynched as recently as the 1940s. Homosexuality was regarded as the worst of sins.

And yet Elvis walked on stage, wearing women's makeup, and waved his groin in the faces of the daughters of those very men. Little wonder there was an outcry.

LEFT A smoldering Elvis reclining at his home in Memphis, '56.

ABOVE It's hard to imagine just how incredible Elvis' stage show was for audiences.

Images Alamy, Getty Images

Most of the controversy took place in 1956, the year when Elvis first came to national and international attention, with two albums in the charts, several live performances, and appearances on radio and TV. Initially, muted complaints were heard simply because he was placed in front of an audience that couldn't understand what he was doing—such as a two-week residency in April at the New Frontier Hotel and Casino in Las Vegas, where the guests were both middle-aged and conservative.

Elvis went down "like a jug of corn liquor at a champagne party," wrote *Newsweek*, essentially because he thrust his nether regions back and forward as he danced. These motions wouldn't raise an eyebrow nowadays, but back in 1956, this stuff was pure dynamite.

Protests about his act became more widely heard when he played in front of teenage audiences, some of whom became genuinely hysterical. We know now that young music fans tend to scream at pop stars for a reason; psychologists have identified it as a

> ## TEENAGERS WHOOPED AT THEIR TV SCREENS; PARENTS WATCHED AGHAST; THE CRITICS WORKED THEMSELVES UP INTO A RIGHTEOUS FRENZY.

bonding ritual, designed to elicit a feeling of community.

"Presley is a definite danger to the security of the United States," frothed a Catholic newspaper in La Crosse, Wisconsin, in a letter to J. Edgar Hoover, director of the FBI. "His actions and motions were such as to rouse the sexual passions of teenaged youth . . . After the show, more than 1,000 teenagers tried to gang into Presley's room at the auditorium . . . Indications of the harm Presley did just in La Crosse were the two

high school girls . . . whose abdomen and thigh had Presley's autograph."

While Elvis should probably have thought twice before signing anyone's anatomy, the fact remains that a ridiculous amount of fuss was being created over the sight of a singer gyrating in an unusual fashion. Had he changed his performance style, the controversy might have died away after a while, but Elvis—no doubt deliberately—chose to amp up his onstage thrustings, most notably on *The Milton Berle Show*, a widely

ABOVE Where Elvis went, you could be sure fans would follow.

ABOVE Elvis' mix of beauty and masculinity was unlike anything at the time.

RIGHT From *G.I. Blues*, in no way harming the sex symbol status.

BELOW The hysteria around Elvis scared the older generation.

watched TV program broadcast on June 5.

Elvis had played on Berle's show before, but this time he left his guitar backstage, choosing to perform unaided—supposedly on the advice of Berle himself, who suggested "Let 'em see you, son." Halfway through singing "Hound Dog," Elvis abruptly halted the uptempo song and launched into a slower version that allowed him to swing his pelvis back and forth. Teenagers whooped at their TV screens; parents watched aghast; the critics worked themselves up into a righteous frenzy.

"Mr. Presley has no discernible singing ability," said the *New York Times*, adding, "His one specialty is an accented movement of the body, primarily identified with the repertoire of the blond bombshells of the burlesque runway." *The New York Daily News* remarked that popular music "has reached its lowest depths in the 'grunt and groin' antics of one Elvis Presley . . . Elvis, who rotates his pelvis . . . gave an exhibition that was suggestive and vulgar, tinged with the kind of animalism that should be confined to dives and bordellos."

TOP From *Girls! Girls! Girls!*, when Elvis was loved by fans, not critics.

LEFT Backstage at *The Milton Berle Show*, where the pelvis went crazy.

RIGHT Much of America had never seen hysteria like this.

And so it went on. Of course, newspapers thrive on controversy and generate it deliberately in order to sell more copies and make money, but still, what Elvis was doing was definitely a) unprecedented, at least for White audiences unfamiliar with African-American music such as jazz and swing, and b) a bit rude.

Commercially, the protests caused by Elvis and his crotch did his career no end of good. He knew how far to take it, too: when he played *The Steve Allen Show* in July, on which he sang to an actual dog during "Hound Dog," he restrained his below-the-belt acrobatics. As he told one reporter, "I'm holding down on this show. I don't want to do anything to make people dislike me. I think TV is important so I'm going to go along, but I won't be able to give the kind of show I do in a personal appearance."

Still, he defended his dancing style, explaining, "I don't feel like I'm doing anything wrong . . . I don't see how any type of music would have any bad influence on people when it's only music . . . I mean, how would rock 'n' roll music make anyone rebel against their parents?" This was a touch naïve, in retrospect, because rock 'n' roll was precisely about rebellion. It was the call of the wild of the new demographic of teenagers who were enjoying newfound economic freedom in America's postwar boom—and, having been too young to fight in World War II, didn't care about the quiet life that their parents craved.

Nonetheless, Elvis' rise to the top wasn't unhindered: the USA's political-religious axis was a powerful enemy, and in no time the establishment lined up, eager to take him down. At one show in Jacksonville, Florida, a local juvenile court judge labeled him a "savage" and promised to arrest him if he did his onstage act: in response, Elvis stood still during the performance—while waggling a finger sarcastically to and fro.

After 1956 the controversy died down, or at least it was less widely reported. There were two reasons for this. First, Elvis toned down his act a little: after his first two albums, his music became more polished and more diverse, with more ballads and less throat-shredding, hip-swinging rock 'n' roll. More importantly, though, we should understand a crucial point in the Presley story: by now, Elvis had won. No petty judge could stand against an artist of his commercial stature. No conservative politician could muster much support against a singer whose music was so widely loved.

With his performances thrilling audiences in ways that had previously been undreamed of, Elvis set a new norm. Whatever you think of his music and his life choices, you have to admit that few musicians have managed to spark a cultural change as seismic as this one. Thanks to Elvis, rock music and sex were now intertwined—permanently.

ABOVE How many teenagers had a room that looked like this?

The ARMY YEARS

In 1958, Elvis headed to Germany to serve his country. Was this to be the end of the line for the rockin' King?

What do you do when you're the most famous singer in the world, with untold wealth and luxury, and you're suddenly told you have to do a day job alongside regular people for the next two years? In the case of Elvis Presley and his manager Colonel Tom Parker, you manage it very carefully—so that when that two years is up, you're even more famous than before.

Told in late 1957 that he would be inducted into the US army on January 20, 1958, Elvis took it in his stride—at least in public. In reality, drama had raged behind the scenes for the previous year, with Colonel Tom and the US armed forces all trying to figure out what to do about the mandatory national service of the biggest star in America.

One possible option was for Elvis to do what was known as "Special Services"—a quick six weeks of basic training, followed by free shows for the soldiers. Colonel Tom rightly realized that Elvis would be the subject of much scorn if he took this easy, celebrity option. Subsequently, both the navy and army offered Elvis special treatment, the former suggesting the formation of a unique "Elvis Presley Company" made up of his buddies, and the latter offering him a gig essentially as a PR guy, touring the world and boosting morale at army bases.

Elvis, or rather Colonel Tom, said no to both options, concluding that the kid was just going to have to endure a regular period of national service alongside the rest of his cohort. "Taking any of these deals will make millions of Americans angry," said Colonel Tom, which

ABOVE A true rock 'n' roll star never leaves his guitar, even on basic training.

LEFT A portrait of a smiling Elvis taken while he was on tour in Germany, 1958.

was certainly an accurate statement, if a little unsympathetic.

After requesting an extension so that he could complete the filming of *King Creole*, Elvis reported for duty on March 24, 1958. He was assigned the number 53310761 and made the leader of his group of new soldiers-in-training, an interesting move that made it clear just how closely his new employers were watching him. His arrival at Fort Chaffee, Arkansas, was a media event, with hundreds of fans in attendance: it seemed that the profile of the hottest young guitar-slinger of the age was unlikely to diminish simply because he wouldn't be appearing on TV for a while.

The first few months of Elvis' national service saw him assigned to Company A of the Third Armored Division's 1st Medium Tank Battalion, located in Fort Hood in Texas. It seems that he did well there, becoming a pistol sharpshooter; he is said to have been a decent soldier, popular with his peers, and generous with his money

LEFT Elvis giving his beloved mother Gladys a kiss, watched by his dad.

BELOW Being sworn into the United States army, along with fellow recruits.

> ## HE OFTEN WROTE TO HIS FRIEND . . . EXPRESSING HOMESICKNESS, WHILE AN ARMY INSTRUCTOR . . . [SAW] ELVIS BREAK DOWN IN TEARS.

without letting his ego get out of control.

However, behind the cheerful public exterior, Elvis was reportedly miserable. He often wrote to his friend Alan Fortas, expressing his homesickness, while an army instructor named Bill Norwood later spoke about seeing Elvis break down in tears while calling home on Norwood's phone. He was only 22, after all, and the pressure of being the world's biggest singer would not have been eased by the extra burden of getting up at the crack of dawn to polish his boots and march around a parade ground.

Elvis' mood improved when he was permitted to live off the base, sharing a house with his parents, grandparents, and a friend, Lamar Fike. The arrangement sounds unusual for a soldier of private rank, but in fact Elvis' family were technically his dependents and so this living situation was approved. Colonel Tom often visited, keeping his client informed about future

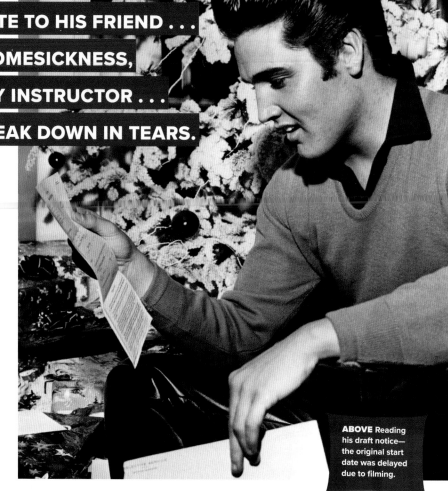

ABOVE Reading his draft notice— the original start date was delayed due to filming.

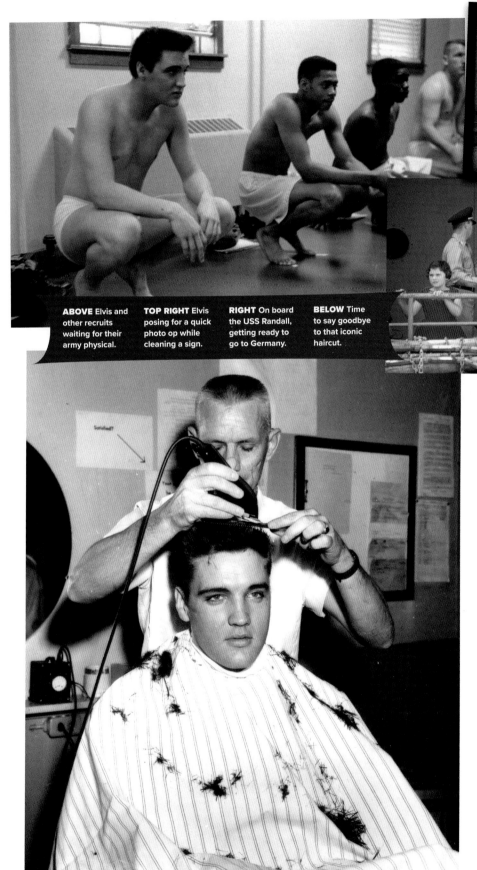

ABOVE Elvis and other recruits waiting for their army physical.

TOP RIGHT Elvis posing for a quick photo op while cleaning a sign.

RIGHT On board the USS Randall, getting ready to go to Germany.

BELOW Time to say goodbye to that iconic haircut.

releases; his plan was that RCA would slowly release a backed up stockpile of singles and LPs over 1958 and 1959, enabling an easy return to public life for Elvis once the army let him go.

Personal tragedy awaited, however. On August 8, Gladys Presley became ill with a deteriorated liver. Her diet, never the most healthy given that she had spent most of her life in extreme poverty, was now made worse by an increased alcohol intake; the booze, it seemed, helped her deal with the unprecedented fame of her son. She also used diet pills—hardly likely to be a healthy option, given the medical practices of the day—and collapsed after an argument with her husband. She was rushed to Memphis where, after some conflict with his superiors, Elvis joined her. Sadly, she was dead within a week, succumbing to cirrhosis on August 14 at the age of only 46. Her cause of death was listed as a heart attack.

The impact on the young Elvis was absolutely devastating—a shock from which he is thought never to have fully recovered. His frame of mind would not have been helped by his introduction around this time to amphetamines, which he liked for the energy boost that they supplied, as well as their assistance with weight loss, a struggle that lasted for the rest of his life.

In September, the grieving singer was posted with the 3rd Armored Division to the town of Friedberg in what was then West Germany. The media gave the trip enormous

> ## "
> # THEY THOUGHT I COULDN'T TAKE IT . . . AND I WAS DETERMINED . . . TO PROVE OTHERWISE, NOT ONLY TO THE PEOPLE WHO WERE WONDERING, BUT TO MYSELF.
> ★ *Elvis Presley*

ABOVE Elvis' training saw him get hands on with artillery guns.

BELOW A press conference in Scotland, after leaving the army.

coverage, although they didn't know what Elvis did when he got to Europe. He turned down another offer of "Special Services," and was himself removed from the post of driver to the commanding officer of Company D, Captain Russell, when that officer grew tired of the constant attention Elvis attracted. Instead, he became a driver for a platoon sergeant called Ira Jones, who later wrote a book about the experience.

Once more living off the base, Elvis and his family retinue first stayed in a hotel called Hilberts in Bad Homburg and then in the Grunewald Hotel in Bad Nauheim. It's interesting to think of the young recruit doing

ABOVE Elvis stands with the other recruits on a military base in Germany, 1958.

LEFT A 16-year-old Priscilla sits writing Elvis a letter.

BELOW Handing his pay to Colonel Tom on the day of his discharge.

tank training by day and retiring to a five-star suite with room service in the evening, while taking calls from his manager in America about his latest single—but that's apparently how his life was at this stage. Finally, Elvis moved to a five-bedroom house in the nearby Goethestrasse, where fans would gather daily to get his autograph.

While stationed in Friedberg, Elvis met his future wife, Priscilla Beaulieu, then only 14. By any standards, then or now, it is bizarre that a 24-year-old man would enter a romantic relationship with a girl a decade his junior. As was so often the case back then, the weirdness of that situation was generally

dismissed – particularly as Priscilla insisted that the relationship remained platonic until their marriage in 1967.

In early 1960, Elvis received word of his honorable discharge from the army, which promoted him to sergeant and gave him a Good Conduct Medal for his efforts. In a farewell press conference on March 1, he explained, "People were expecting me to mess up, to goof up in one way or another. They thought I couldn't take it and so forth, and I was determined to go to any limits to prove otherwise, not only to the people who were wondering, but to myself."

His flight home the following day included a

stop at Prestwick Airport in Scotland to refuel, his only visit to the UK, and was met by a crowd of fans and celebs including Nancy Sinatra. RCA also sent representatives, eager to make it obvious that the King would be continuing his interrupted recording career as soon as possible, and on March 5, Elvis was honorably discharged from the army.

Within days, he was back in the studio, his public profile restored and healthy. Elvis was a decorated servant of his country now, with all hints of establishment-baiting rebellion in the past. Would this new profile be a boost to his career, or would it be his downfall?

Images Getty Images

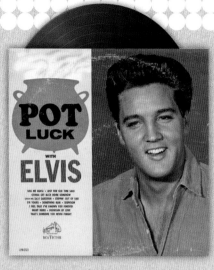

POT LUCK

Released **May 1962**

Better than its title implies, but still not up to Kingly standards.

I t's a shame that this album's title implies that its contents are leftovers. In fact, Elvis' last non-soundtrack LP for the next seven years is a mostly decent collection of songs, as well as a kind of resigned nod to the fact that as a singer, the movie industry was inevitably where Elvis would spend most of the sixties.

High points are obvious to anyone prepared to take a serious listen. "Gonna Get Back Home Somehow" is never mentioned in any list of superior Elvis songs, but it should be, as should "(Such An) Easy Question" and *Pot Luck*'s best-known cut, "Suspicion." Listen to "She's Not You" on the 1999 reissue, not because it's a showstopping song but because it showcases a relatively new singing approach for Elvis—the softer style introduced on "Can't Help Falling in Love."

Reviews seem to indicate that one of this album's songs, "That's Someone You Never Forget," was cowritten by Elvis—and they do actually mean cowritten, rather than merely having a Presley credit stuck onto it so he and his manager could earn more money. If this is truly the case, then Elvis had more to him as a writer than he's given credit for, as it's a haunting song with memorable gospel touches.

Still, the truth is that any of these mid-career Elvis albums are populated with substandard songs compared to those recorded at his peak. In *Pot Luck*'s case, the tracks to skip are "I Feel That I've Known You Forever," "Just For Old Time Sake," and "I'm Yours," which will only grab the attention of the most ardent Presley disciple. There's gold here, but you need to dig deep to find it.

TRACKLIST

SIDE ONE

1. Kiss Me Quick
2. Just for Old Time Sake
3. Gonna Get Back Home Somehow
4. (Such an) Easy Question
5. Steppin' Out of Line
6. I'm Yours

SIDE TWO

1. Something Blue
2. Suspicion
3. I Feel That I've Known You Forever
4. Night Rider
5. Fountain of Love
6. That's Someone You Never Forget

LEFT Working hard on a soundtrack for a movie.

ABOVE Performing with Tommy and Jimmy Dorsey.

RIGHT Still from *Girls! Girls! Girls!*, released April 1962.

ELVIS FOR EVERYONE!

Released August 1965

Ignore the shoddy artwork and throwaway title—there are some vintage delights on this LP.

Sometimes you wonder if anyone at RCA actually cared about quality control when it came to the career of their once and future King, Elvis. It's not that the music on *Elvis For Everyone!* is bad, because it absolutely isn't. The problem is that the title and cover make it clear that this LP was thrown together from various eras of Elvis' career.

Still, get over this not-inconsiderable hurdle and there's plenty to enjoy here, making the LP's title at least a reasonable one in that sense. Spend some time with "Tomorrow Night," a Sun-recorded song that was 10 years old when this album was compiled: the raw passion of the young truck driver who sang it is refreshing to hear from the perspective of the over-indulged mid-sixties Presley.

There's 1958's "Your Cheatin' Heart" to enjoy, too, and a joyous run-through of Chuck Berry's "Memphis, Tennessee." Who knows what the middle-aged audiences who went to see Elvis in Vegas thought of simple rock songs such as this one, but from today's point of view these old songs sound absolutely colossal. See also an old blues from '57 titled "When It Rains, It Really Pours," on which our man does his signature trick of making you feel what he's feeling.

Of course, once you've enjoyed these ancient cuts you're left with a stack of insipid pop songs and ballads to get through. A lot of people love these songs, and indeed there are a couple of heartfelt cuts to enjoy in that style: "Summer Kisses, Winter Tears" and "Forget Me Never" are two examples. Compared to the ultra-badass fifties songs, though, the later stuff can't help but sound a little weak.

TOP LEFT Just another typical day when you're Elvis Presley.

ABOVE Elvis with costar Ann-Margret in 1965's *Viva Las Vegas*.

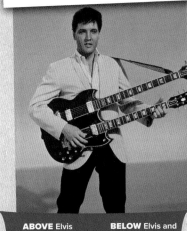

ABOVE Elvis with double bass, which he played in *Spinout*.

BELOW Elvis and Sinatra snapped sharing a joke in Hollywood, '65.

TRACKLIST

SIDE ONE

1 Your Cheatin' Heart
2 Summer Kisses, Winter Tears
3 Finders Keepers, Losers Weepers
4 In My Way
5 Tomorrow Night
6 Memphis, Tennessee

SIDE TWO

1 For the Millionth and the Last Time
2 Forget Me Never
3 Sound Advice
4 Santa Lucia
5 I Met Her Today
6 When It Rains, It Really Pours

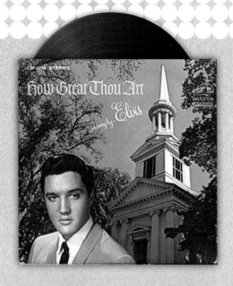

HOW GREAT THOU ART

Released **February 1967**

Elvis' second album of gospel music came with added rock 'n' roll. Does the combination actually work?

LEFT A still of Elvis taken from the 1967 film, *Clambake*.

ABOVE Another film from 1967, this time it's *Double Trouble*.

BELOW 1967 was a busy year for Elvis—he also got married!

You can imagine the suits' reaction at RCA when Elvis and Colonel Tom proposed a second album of gospel music. Sure, the first one, *His Hand In Mine* had done just fine back in 1960—but this was '67, when the kids were taking acid and protesting against the war in Vietnam. The answer that someone— Elvis himself, perhaps—came up with was to include some rockin' versions of gospel tunes on the new collection.

If this idea sounds awful on paper, never fear: it worked in practice. Mostly, anyway: when you hear Elvis dive into "So High" and "By and By," you realize what he was getting at. It helps if you remember where Elvis came from: a poverty-stricken upbringing in America's South, where religion was a source of spiritual refreshment, of physical excitement, and pretty much the only thing that saved most people from giving up altogether. This explains the

rocked-up bite of "Run On," which you could comfortably place among Elvis' Sun sides, such is its uptempo energy.

Flip the record and you're given a whole load of Elvis balladry, where he intones his Christian convictions in a serious, sober style. Whether you sympathize with his beliefs or not, take a moment to absorb the atmosphere of these songs, delivered by a man whose immersion in their sentiments was obviously both genuine and deep. The title cut sees him on amazing vocal form, the strength of his voice giving the song power, and although "In the Garden" is just Elvis plus church organ, it's completely convincing. The LP finishes with "Where No One Stands Alone" and the famous "Crying in the Chapel," in which everything you need to know about Elvis and his relationship with his God is laid bare. It's powerful stuff, wherever you stand.

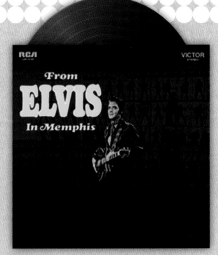

FROM ELVIS IN MEMPHIS

Released June 1969

A stone-cold masterpiece, the Memphis album is the one to revisit for the very best of Presley.

LEFT Doing his stuff at his second home—Las Vegas, 1969.

ABOVE A cheeky shot after a press conference.

RIGHT At his first show in Vegas for over 13 years.

BELOW Looking relaxed after his '69 Vegas press conference.

TRACKLIST

SIDE ONE

1 Wearin' That Loved On Look
2 Only the Strong Survive
3 I'll Hold You in My Heart (Till I Can Hold You in My Arms)
4 Long Black Limousine
5 It Keeps Right On A-Hurtin'
6 I'm Movin' On

SIDE TWO

1 Power of My Love
2 Gentle on My Mind
3 After Loving You
4 True Love Travels on a Gravel Road
5 Any Day Now
6 In the Ghetto

Even all these years later, you can practically still hear Elvis' die-hard fans punching the air and shouting "finally!" when *From Elvis in Memphis* finished playing on their Victrola turntables. After years of soundtracks and pop, their man had delivered his best album since the Sun years.

The LP is best described as white soul, or blue-eyed soul in the language of the day, but it pulls in influences from blues, funk, and country too, making for a heady brew. Elvis had partnered with producer Chips Moman and some of the finest session musicians of all time at American Studios in Memphis, and the results spoke for themselves.

If you were looking for powerful, bluesy rock 'n' roll, you had it in "Power of My Love" and "After Loving You"; if it was a funked-up soul jam you needed, you had "Wearin' That Loved On Look." Crisp, snappy pop tunes came in the form of "Gentle on My Mind" and "Long Black Limousine," the latter blending country, gospel, and blues. "In the Ghetto," a "message song," followed up the *'68 Special*'s "If I Can Dream," while "It Keeps Right On A-Hurtin" paid tribute to traditional country and western. There was also an excellent Burt Bacharach cover, "Any Day Now," and a silky ballad, "True Love Travels on a Gravel Road."

What was most exciting was that Elvis sounded as if he believed in himself again, and what's more, that he believed he could be as exciting as he had been a decade before.

Images Elvis Presley (album covers), Getty Images, Alamy

61

FROM MEMPHIS TO VEGAS / FROM VEGAS TO MEMPHIS

Released **October 1969**

One album of live magic, another of studio snoozing—a reminder of the King's true talents.

I n 1969, Elvis was on such incredible form that RCA's decision to release a double LP—one live, one studio—seems adventurous rather than unwise, as it would have been at any point afterward. The label and Colonel Tom may well have liked the idea because it gave them the chance to reissue each album independently, of course, and indeed this did come to pass.

From Memphis To Vegas / From Vegas To Memphis is a mighty document of the King at the high point of his reign. The live album is by far the better one, kicking off with familiar old songs to remind you how good Elvis was on stage at this point. The one-two of "Blue Suede Shoes" and "Johnny B. Goode" is unsurpassable, and a sped-up version of "All Shook Up" is full of energy, even though Elvis is audibly puffed by the end.

Kudos to his band members James Burton (guitar), Jerry Scheff (bass), and Ronnie Tutt (drums) who compete against a 40-piece orchestra and two sets of backing singers. On "Are You Lonesome Tonight?" Whitney Houston's mother Cissy, delivers some mighty-lunged wailing. Listen out for a huge, seven-minute version of "Suspicious Minds," and remember just how astonishing this band was.

The studio album, although decent enough, doesn't match up to the two glorious sides of live songs. Your best bets are probably "This is the Story," "Without Love (There is Nothing)," and "Do You Know Who I Am?"—but if you needed proof that Elvis excelled on stage rather than in the studio, this is it. The studio cuts are catchy and interesting—but live? The man was pure dynamite.

LEFT Snaps from the International Hotel 1969 Vegas shows.

ABOVE The Vegas shows were a triumph for Elvis.

TRACKLIST

SIDE ONE

1 Blue Suede Shoes
2 Johnny B. Goode
3 All Shook Up
4 Are You Lonesome Tonight?
5 Hound Dog
6 I Can't Stop Loving You
7 My Babe

SIDE TWO

1 Mystery Train/Tiger Man
2 Words
3 In the Ghetto
4 Suspicious Minds
5 Can't Help Falling In Love

SIDE THREE

1 Inherit the Wind
2 This is the Story
3 Stranger in My Own Home Town
4 A Little Bit of Green
5 And the Grass Won't Pay No Mind

SIDE FOUR

1 Do You Know Who I Am?
2 From a Jack to a King
3 The Fair's Moving On
4 You'll Think of Me
5 Without Love (There is Nothing)

THAT'S THE WAY IT IS

Released **November 1970**

The non-soundtrack to the documentary film merged studio and live tracks.

LEFT *That's the Way It Is* documented Elvis live.

MIDDLE The shows of this era captured Elvis at his peak.

ABOVE Who else could combine a jumpsuit with a cape?

TRACKLIST

SIDE ONE

1 I Just Can't Help Believin'
2 Twenty Days and Twenty Nights
3 How the Web Was Woven
4 Patch It Up
5 Mary in the Morning
6 You Don't Have to Say You Love Me

SIDE TWO

1 You've Lost That Lovin' Feelin'
2 I've Lost You
3 Just Pretend
4 Stranger in the Crowd
5 The Next Step Is Love
6 Bridge Over Troubled Water

That's the Way It Is is a decent album in its own right, sharing a title with a 1970 documentary covering Elvis' return to live performance, but more than that, it's the sound of the great man entering the third and final phase of his career. No, that doesn't mean that it follows up the Hillbilly Cat of the fifties and the King of Hollywood of the sixties with jumpsuits, rhinestones, and poor health—far from it.

Lean, relaxed, in good humor, and pretty much at the peak of his form, Elvis steps up on this album into a range of territories with ease and panache. He's assisted here by a phenomenal studio band, with whom he could go toe-to-toe when it came to work ethic and an ability to internalize the songs. One-third of the LP sees him live on stage in Las Vegas, from then on his spiritual home, while the rest of it was recorded in Nashville.

The latter tracks hit home best, with Elvis emoting persuasively on "How the Web Was Woven," "Just Pretend," and "Stranger in the Crowd," while "Twenty Days and Twenty Nights" is a soaring ballad with effortless harmony vocals. Quieter songs such as this one allow Elvis the space to back off a little, a welcome step: if you're after fireworks, then the fuller dimensions of his version of "Bridge Over Troubled Water" will be your best starting point.

On this album, Elvis is audibly enjoying himself, a relief to hear at this relatively late stage in his career. It's the sound of the King relishing his time at the top, before fashions squeezed him out of vogue and the depressing elements of life eventually wore him down.

Elvis in HOLLYWOOD

Elvis was the King of the silver screen as well as of the stage—but were his movies as bad as everyone thinks?

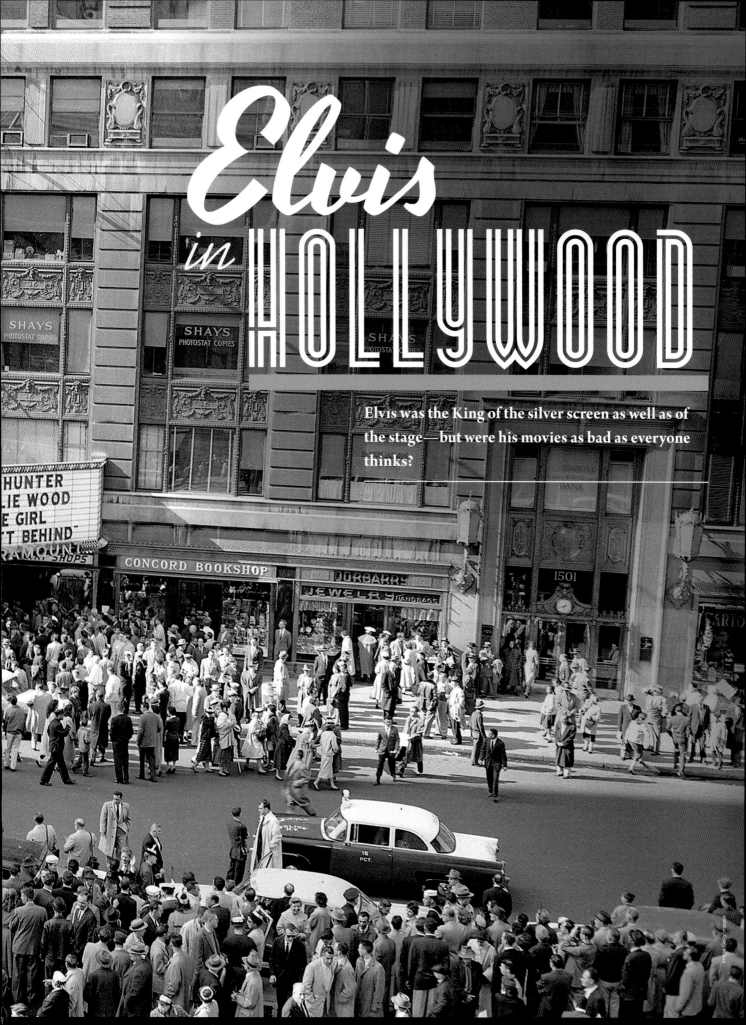

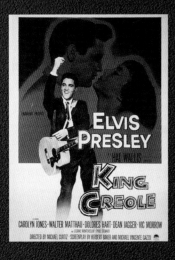

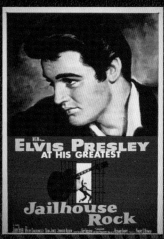

E

lvis Presley acted in 31 films—in the sense of playing fictional parts in cinematic movies, rather than playing himself in concert or documentary productions. Take a deep breath—here comes the full, 31-movie roll call: *Love Me Tender* (1956), *Loving You* and *Jailhouse Rock* (both 1957), *King Creole* (1958), *G.I. Blues* and *Flaming Star* (both 1960, after a two-year break for Elvis' national service), *Wild in the Country* and *Blue Hawaii* (both 1961), *Follow That Dream, Kid Galahad,* and *Girls! Girls! Girls!* (all 1962), *It Happened at the World's Fair* and *Fun in Acapulco* (both 1963), and *Kissin' Cousins, Viva Las Vegas* (aka *Love in Las Vegas*), and *Roustabout* (all filmed in 1964).

These were followed by *Girl Happy, Tickle Me,* and *Harum Scarum* (all 1965), *Frankie and Johnny, Paradise, Hawaiian Style,* and *Spinout* (all 1966), *Easy Come, Easy Go, Double Trouble,* and *Clambake* (all 1967), *Stay Away, Joe, Speedway,* and *Live a Little, Love a Little* (all 1968) and *Charro!, The Trouble With Girls,* and *Change of Habit* (all 1969).

Got all that? Now, let's note that of the 31 films, 12 were made by Metro-Goldwyn-Mayer, nine by Paramount, four by United Artists, three by 20th Century Fox, and one each by Universal, Allied Artists, and National General.

Elvis was sought after throughout Hollywood, it seemed, free to move from studio to studio as he—and his manager Colonel Tom—chose. Records indicate that all the movies, with one notable exception, made decent money. Wouldn't anyone envy Elvis his second career as a movie star?

Well, let's look at that for a moment. If you dig into the Presley chronology, it turns out that Elvis was interested in acting before many people had ever heard of him as a singer: a few weeks before "Heartbreak Hotel" was a smash hit in 1956, he had attended a screen test for his first role, a supporting part in *Love Me Tender.* He is said to have admired the actors James Dean, Tony Curtis, and Marlon Brando in his youth, watching their films and reciting their lines while working as a theater usher. One of his first requests to his hardheaded manager,

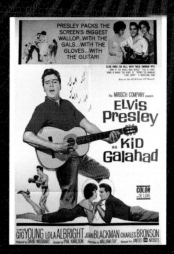

THE TRAGEDY IS THAT ELVIS COULD PROBABLY HAVE PULLED OFF SOME SERIOUS ACTING JOBS IF HE'D BEEN GIVEN THE CHANCE: HE CERTAINLY HAD THE WILL.

Colonel Tom, was that he embark on an acting career in parallel with his music.

There's no doubt, then, that Elvis was attracted to the bright lights of Hollywood. His perennial problem, which is the same one faced by any musician who wants to act, is that people tend not to take such ambitions seriously, in much the same way they don't when

actors express an interest in recording music.

The tragedy is that Elvis could probably have pulled off some serious acting jobs if he'd been given the chance: he certainly had the will, at least in the early days. After a screen test for the producer Hal Wallis at Paramount Studios on March 26, 1956, Wallis'

partner, Joe Hazen, stated, "As a straight actor, the guy has great potentialities," while a drama coach, Charlotte Clary, revealed to her students, "Now that is a natural born actor."

Elvis sometimes talked about studying at the famed Actors Studio in New York, the home of method acting, and he was perfectly clear in his mind that he didn't want to sing in any films, in order to be taken seriously as an actor. The first of these ideas never materialized, presumably for scheduling reasons, and Elvis was talked out of the latter conviction by Colonel Tom, who decided that both the music and the movies would sell better if each promoted the other.

This was proven when the *Love Me Tender* film, song, and EP all made huge sums of money. One or two critics gave it their begrudging approval, with the *Los Angeles Times* remarking: "Elvis can

LEFT Elvis' movies attracted the same screaming audiences as his concerts.

ABOVE 1957's *Loving You* was Elvis' second movie and his first in color.

LEFT A promo shot for *Jailhouse Rock*, in which Elvis played a convict with a dream.

ABOVE From *King Creole*, where the 23-year-old Elvis acted the part of a high school student.

act . . . the boy's real good." Not that reviewers would have been able to hear what was actually being said on the silver screen, as Elvis' friend Jerry Schilling later recalled. "The screams of the girls around me made it just about impossible to follow the story," he wrote. "This was the first time I'd seen an audience treat a film like it was a live concert, loudly responding to every move made and word uttered by their favorite star."

In the wake of this early success, the die was essentially cast. Wallis had given Elvis a highly flexible contract for seven films, allowing him to make a movie for other studios if he so wished, and the money flowed right in. *Love Me Tender* made a comfortable $4 million at the box office, about four times its budget, and

so did the next couple of Presley vehicles: *Loving You* and *Jailhouse Rock*. Sure, the roles Elvis played were undemanding— the brother of a Confederate soldier, a band leader, and a convict who dreams of becoming a star—but Wallis had promised to find Elvis some more serious roles, and at least some of the music, particularly in *Jailhouse Rock*, was solid stuff.

Once *King Creole* came out in 1958 and showed off Elvis' acting chops, with the 23-year-old singer successfully persuading audiences that he could play a high school student, the template was established. From now on, his films would be slight comedies with musical elements and a central character, played by Elvis, who fought, sang, and seduced his way out of various situations.

This in itself would not have been so bad, had the quality of the film scripts and the music that accompanied them not sunk so spectacularly low over the next couple of years. In the end, the studio teams perfected the art of shooting and editing a given Presley film in just 17 days, degrading Elvis' talents and diminishing his critical profile in doing so.

Tragically, his movie career could have been so different: he is said to have been offered the chance to audition for *The Godfather, Cat on a Hot Tin Roof, The Defiant Ones, Midnight Cowboy, A Star is Born* and *West Side Story*—but Colonel Tom advised against them. All these films ultimately provided Academy Awards for their stars, which must have been particularly galling for the man who once dreamed of attending the Actors Studio.

After a while, Elvis simply sank into apathy, accepting the cheesy roles without question as they came along. As his lifelong friend Red West said of the movies: "I enjoyed the first ones. *Blue Hawaii, G.I. Blues, Flaming Star* especially. I could count on one hand the ones that were good, and the rest of them were things that were thrown at him with no thought of anything other than making a buck . . . Elvis just kinda breezed through the others to get them out of the way, because there was nothing to them as far as he was concerned. *Wild in the Country* was some of the best acting without a doubt he ever did, and the one in New Orleans— *King Creole*—those were two."

ABOVE Elvis considered *Blue Hawaii* a film that did well for him.

RIGHT A few years after *Blue Hawaii* came *Paradise, Hawaiian Style*.

FAR RIGHT A still from *Wild in the Country*.

LEFT Getting in a bust up over someone trying to steal his girl in *Girls! Girls! Girls!*.

ABOVE Surrounded by three sets of twins, who were needed for filming *G.I. Blues*.

Let's be objective about these films, if that's possible after so long. Are they all bad? A reasonable answer is no—not entirely. Take *Flaming Star* from 1960, in which Elvis plays a mixed-race rancher caught between White settlers and Native Americans. On his insistence, only two songs were included, and he performed those in character rather than as the familiar hip-swinging rocker. Critics praised his "brooding presence" and his progress as an actor, although they weren't quite ready to give him a rave review.

Then there's *Wild in the Country* from 1961, in which Elvis finally got the chance to play a serious, dramatic role, albeit one who has to sing four songs for no obvious reason. His troubled character describes a complex arc, and Elvis took direction well in order to enable his portrayal. Unfortunately, the critics gave it a kicking, but not because Elvis didn't do his job: they seemed to feel that the film itself was a disappointment, and not solely because of its leading man. The star, who is said to have pocketed $300,000—almost 10 times that now—would never play another serious role.

Unfortunately, it only went downhill

" **ELVIS JUST KIND OF BREEZED THROUGH THE OTHERS TO GET THEM OUT OF THE WAY, BECAUSE THERE WAS NOTHING TO THEM.**

★ *Red West*

from there, with Elvis losing interest in almost every aspect of whatever film he was engaged on. His 1967 film *Clambake* is routinely cited as one of his very worst, not least by Elvis himself, who admitted that he did it only for the paycheck. Perhaps if the movie, which relied heavily on faked shots of Elvis water-skiing—sometimes dressed in an unlikely blouson—had come out in the late fifties, when the cult of Presley was at its peak, it might have received a warmer reception. By 1967, young moviegoers expected more for their buck, given that popular culture was engaged elsewhere in real-world struggles such as civil rights and the war in Vietnam.

Despite the occasional moderate filmic success, the scales soon fell from Elvis' eyes. The acting dream was effectively over for him, although the films were still making him richer. By the mid-sixties he was

> ## " I SURE LOST MY DIRECTION IN HOLLYWOOD. MY SONGS WERE THE SAME CONVEYOR-BELT MASS PRODUCTION, JUST LIKE MOST OF MY MOVIES WERE.
>
> ★ *Elvis Presley*

ABOVE Performing on a ladder in the 1964 film *Roustabout*.

LEFT An almost unrecognizable Elvis in *Charro!*.

trapped on a ridiculous treadmill, making two or more lightweight movies a year while his musical talents languished. By the end of the decade, he'd had enough and was determined to return to the stage: when his acting contracts expired in 1969, they were not renewed.

As Elvis told a press conference in Las Vegas the same year: "I did some good pictures that did very well for me, like *Blue Hawaii*. . . and some pretty forgettable ones too! I sure lost my musical direction in Hollywood. My songs were the same conveyor-belt mass production, just like most of my movies were. Now I'm back and on the right road. Those movies sure got me into a rut. I want to make amends. I really missed working live, in front of an audience, that's why I'm here."

Fortunately, he retained a sense of humor about it all. As John Lennon later put it:

"It was nice meeting Elvis. . . I asked him if he was preparing new ideas for his next film, and he drawled, 'Ah sure am. Ah play a country boy with a guitar who meets a few gals along the way, and ah sing a few songs.' We all looked at one another. Finally Presley and Colonel Parker laughed and explained that the only time they departed from that formula—for *Wild in the Country*—they lost money!"

By the early seventies, Elvis' career as a leading man seemed like a bygone era. Rejuvenated as a singer and on excellent form until around 1975, he looked back on those lost years in studio lots with a combination of regret and amusement. The real question is what he would have

gone on to do, filmically speaking, had he cleaned up his lifestyle and achieved a full lifespan. By his forties, Elvis' face was interesting rather than merely pretty, and expressive rather than simply attractive. In his fifties and beyond, it's not hard to imagine that he could have gone on to be a serious character actor, like many of his contemporaries.

Still, this is a fantasy as insubstantial as the characters Elvis played in his twenties and thirties. It's a shame that he wasted so much time chasing the Hollywood dream, when he already had all the success he could ever have dreamed of as a singer. There's a lesson for us all there.

in CONCERT

Meet the King where he's happiest—tearing it up on stage in his most memorable performances.

LEFT Elvis in the early years (1956), in front of a poster of his Las Vegas show.

ABOVE All the sparkle of later years still couldn't hide Elvis' talent.

I f Elvis Presley had survived until today, he might well have been reminiscing here about his long and chaotic career as a stage performer, no doubt with a mischievous glint in his eye and chuckling at some of the antics he got up to. He's not here, though, so in his absence let's celebrate his vast live performance record and raise a glass to some of his best, most influential, most memorable—and downright disastrous—concerts.

The numbers alone are worth bearing in mind. Sources generally agree that Elvis performed 1,684 concerts, between a show in Memphis on July 17, 1954, and his final gig in Indianapolis nearly 23 years later on June 26, 1977. That number excludes informal performances for family and friends or casual jams that were never recorded. He performed in 238 different towns and cities, all in the USA apart from three in Canada, and in many

of those cities he performed many times—46 times in Shreveport, Louisiana, thanks to its *Louisiana Hayride* radio show; 33 times in Memphis; 16 shows in Houston; and hundreds in Las Vegas alone.

Isolating key performances from those 1,684 gigs is subjective but possible. His career as a live performer can be split into two sections: before and after Hollywood. If it's the Hillbilly Cat of the fifties you prefer—naive, raw, vocally untutored, but sexual dynamite—then consider these two.

On July 30, 1954, the 19-year-old Elvis played a set at the Overton Park Shell in Memphis. Backed by Scotty Moore and Bill Black, the event poster billed him as "Ellis Presley" in tiny letters under the name of the main act, Slim Whitman. Nerves and excitement prompted Elvis to start shaking his legs, in a move that was later dubbed "Rubber Legs" by the press. The wide, pleated trousers

LEFT Elvis and Colonel Tom being protected by police while in Hawaii.

BELOW Elvis gives the front row what they came for during an early show.

he was wearing amplified the movement, causing the young women in attendance to shriek in appreciation. While Moore and Black were bemused at this reaction, the young Elvis evidently knew exactly what he was doing—although the thought that he was single-handedly starting a cultural revolution probably didn't occur to him.

Seven years and one day later, Elvis ended the first phase of his live career—which had been overtaken by acting in miserably bad films—with a fundraising show in Honolulu, Hawaii, on March 25, 1961. The objective was to raise money for an ongoing initiative to construct a memorial to the USS Arizona, the warship destroyed in the Pearl Harbor attacks 20 years previously, with the loss of over 1,100 service personnel. It's thought that Colonel Tom came up with the idea of the show after reading about the fundraising efforts: he commented on the event that Elvis, at 26 years old, was similar in age to the men lost on the Arizona, making the fundraiser all the more appropriate.

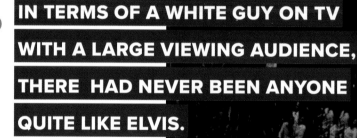

" IN TERMS OF A WHITE GUY ON TV WITH A LARGE VIEWING AUDIENCE, THERE HAD NEVER BEEN ANYONE QUITE LIKE ELVIS.

ABOVE Three shots showing the typical fan response to seeing Elvis on the stage.

RIGHT At a 1969 show in Vegas, a city he played hundreds of shows in.

FAR RIGHT A poster for a 1965 concert, with someone other than Elvis headlining.

STARRING
W S M GRAND OLE OPRY
HANK SNOW
with the RAINBOW RANCH BOYS
SPECIAL ADDED ATTRACTIONS
SLIM WHITMAN
and the STAR DUSTERS
ELVIS PRESLEY
with BILL & SCOTTY
DAVIS SISTERS · ONIE WHEELER
EXTRA SPECIAL
JIMMIE RODGERS SNOW
SHRINE AUD.
NEW BERN - N. C. 2 SHOWS 7:00 & 9:00 P. M.

Elvis, only briefly out of the armed services himself, was deemed a suitable candidate for the event by the powers that be and the event was arranged to take place in Honolulu, conveniently just before Elvis started filming a movie there. What's interesting is that the now establishment-friendly singer reverted to rock 'n' roll type very quickly, pulling off stunts such as a six-foot slide on his knees during "Hound Dog."

"When Elvis came on, the teenagers screamed for two and a half minutes without let-up," commented a local newspaper the next day. "Elvis was wearing his famous gold jacket with the silvery glints like sequins, dark-blue trousers, and a white shirt, and a blue string tie. He wiggles as much as he ever did. The army didn't make him a bit conservative."

You really needed to be there to appreciate the impact of the young Elvis, but unless you're now over 80 years old and lived in Tennessee as a kid, you weren't, so *YouTube* is your best bet. Find any of the shows listed here, or indeed any

high-quality footage of Elvis from around this time, and you'll soon realize just how significant his arrival on the rock 'n' roll scene of the day was. His overtly suggestive stage moves, pretty tame by today's standards but wonderfully shocking in the fifties, had been introduced to Black audiences by Little Richard in 1953 and 1954, but in terms of a White guy on TV with a large viewing audience, there had never been anyone like Elvis.

If you're looking for key shows at the other end of his career, there are many to choose from—although we should be clear that 1969 to 1975 is where he shone most brightly, as the last two years of his life were dogged by ill health and lackluster performances. Before the three Ds—drugs, depression, and divorce—robbed Elvis of his vitality and then of his life, he was still the King of his domain, as the shows we've identified remind us.

Much has been made over the years of the fact that Elvis was overweight in his later life, but this wasn't a major issue before 1975.

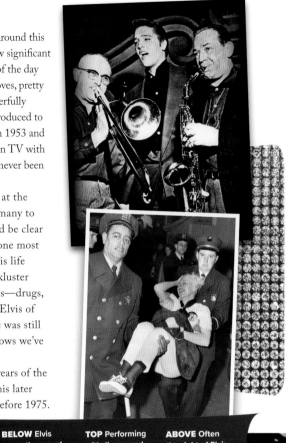

BELOW Elvis wows the crowd during his *Aloha from Hawaii* show.

TOP Performing with Jimmy and Tommy Dorsey on their show.

ABOVE Often the sight of Elvis on stage was too much for fans.

Sure, when he returned to the stage as a 35-year-old in 1970 he couldn't leap around the stage with the panther-like panache of 1956—but even so, he was mostly trim, energetic, and in full control. Yes, the karate moves he introduced to the act look a bit silly by today's standards, but back then, the public hadn't endured 50 years of terrible martial arts movies, and the sight of Elvis sparring and posing was genuinely new.

Where do we start with this period? Perhaps on June 10, 1972, when Elvis flew to New York City to perform four sold-out gigs at Madison Square Garden. He was the first performer to sell out the venue, and a live album called *Elvis: As Recorded at Madison Square Garden* went triple platinum. Or maybe we should consider *Aloha from Hawaii*, a show at the Honolulu International Center on January 14, 1973, when Elvis became the first solo artist to broadcast a live show to the world via satellite. Colonel Tom claimed that more than a billion viewers watched it, although there's no real way of verifying this.

Then, of course, there's Elvis' biggest grossing show ever—a set on New Year's Eve, 1975, in front of 60,000 screaming fans at the Pontiac Silverdome in Michigan. Beginning with "Also Sprach Zarathustra" from *2001: A Space Odyssey*, a suitably melodramatic intro, Elvis played a whole set of hits before counting in 1976 with "'Auld Lang Syne."

In the interests of balance, we need to reflect on one of Elvis' poorer shows, performed almost at the end of his life. On June 21, 1977, he played at Rapid City, South Dakota, even though his demeanor suggested that he should have been at home in bed. Sweaty, overweight, and muttering incoherently, the King was a shadow of his former self, although he surprised everyone at one point with a solo piano-and-vocal rendition of the Righteous Brothers' "Unchained Melody." Fortunately someone pressed record, committing the breathtaking performance for posterity. Two months later, he was gone.

The conclusion? Perhaps that Elvis Presley never lived life as fully as he did when he was on stage. A consummate performer, he even had a concert scheduled for the day he died. Will any of us be as dedicated to our craft?

" ELVIS BECAME THE FIRST SOLO ARTIST TO EVER BROADCAST A LIVE SHOW TO THE WORLD VIA SATELLITE.

TOP Las Vegas would become like a second home to Elvis.

MIDDLE From a 1977 show, just four months before his death.

ABOVE Elvis on stage with his father Vernon in June 1977.

RIGHT Performing to an excited hometown crowd in Tupelo, 1956.

The KING RETURNS

**Back with a vengeance in 1968—but could Elvis
sustain this momentum into the seventies?**

ABOVE Elvis in the *'68 Comeback Special*, the TV program that reinvented him.

RIGHT Elvis had slimmed down for the *Comeback Special* and looked great.

As we've seen, the career of Elvis Presley is often divided into three broad phases—the hot young rock 'n' roller of the fifties, whose early fire was quenched by two years in the army; the insipid movie star of the sixties; and an initially promising seventies, that was tragically cut short. Although logic would dictate otherwise, in some ways it's actually the second phase that is the saddest, because Elvis spent the most creative decade of them all locked into a pattern of making films, rather than fulfilling his true musical potential.

One huge factor in Elvis' favor, however, was that he voluntarily kicked all the Hollywood nonsense to the curb in 1968, reinstating himself in the public eye with the comeback to end all comebacks. This took skill, it took determination, and it most certainly took courage. Elvis rose to the challenge, underwent a rebirth in time for the dawn of the seventies—and made some of his best music in years.

We're talking, of course, about the NBC TV program *Singer Presents . . . Elvis*, broadcast on December 3, 1968, and usually referred to informally as the *'68 Comeback Special*. This cultural milestone came about when Colonel Tom, aware that his client's movie career was essentially at an end, approached NBC with the idea of a Christmas television showcase for Elvis. NBC's producer Bob Finkel liked the idea and persuaded Singer, the sewing machine

> ## ELVIS IS CHARISMATIC— A FACT WHICH AUDIENCES HAD FORGOTTEN, HAVING STOPPED TAKING HIM SERIOUSLY AFTER 1963.

TOP The set of the *Comeback Special* was dramatic.

LEFT The Elvis in 1968 was a different beast to cheesy film Elvis.

ABOVE Carefully framed shots helped make the *Comeback Special*.

RIGHT He may have been over 30, but Elvis was cool once more.

manufacturer, to sponsor the show, as well as refocusing the content on new music by Elvis, rather than Christmas carols.

The whole point of the *'68 Comeback Special* was to redefine Elvis as cool again, a major undertaking given his age—33, ancient by pop standards—and his perceived status as the king of cheesy movies. An appropriately with-it director, Steve Binder, was tasked with making Elvis hip once more, and although Binder had reservations, he pulled it off. His success was due to great set design, stark, tightly framed visuals, and most importantly, a killer look for Elvis himself, slimmed down for the occasion and clad entirely in black leather.

Watch the show on *YouTube* if you haven't done so already. Elvis is charismatic—a fact which audiences at the time had forgotten, having stopped taking him seriously after about 1963. He performs a range of songs

from across his career, jokes with his band—admittedly, some of the banter was pre-written—and talks movingly about the recent murders of Robert F. Kennedy and Martin Luther King. It took four hours to tape the show, edited down to 50 minutes for broadcast.

Audiences loved the *'68 Comeback Special*, and even the critics grudgingly tolerated it—a huge result for Elvis at this point in his career. It was America's most-watched broadcast that week, with 42 percent of the viewing audience tuning in to see Elvis do his stuff. The soundtrack went gold, leading Elvis to leap at the idea of further recording sessions: he had proven that the public still enjoyed his music and was understandably determined to maximize the opportunity.

In some ways, the years of 1968 to 1971 are Elvis' very best, even more so than his

Sun Studios period. Handsome, mostly healthy, and initially happy, he bestrode those recording sessions, creating dozens of great songs over the months and years following his comeback. The first key album of that era was *From Elvis in Memphis* in 1969, where he entered country and soul territory for the first time, with his single "In the Ghetto" becoming his first non-gospel Top 10 hit in six years. The career-defining "Suspicious Minds" followed, the next in a line of hit singles.

The next task was to get back on the road. Overseas offers came in, with the London Palladium offering $28,000 for a one-week engagement, but Elvis was unable to take them, reportedly because Colonel Tom, an illegal immigrant into the USA, was afraid to leave the country. Instead, Las Vegas beckoned, booking him for 57 shows over four weeks in the summer of 1969.

It's at this point that the late-career Elvis cliché begins, largely because he started to wear the famous white jumpsuit for these and subsequent Vegas stints. Make no mistake, though—those early shows in the City of Sin were dynamite, with the King performing at the peak of his powers to packed houses and solid reviews. Attendance records were broken; great albums were recorded; incomprehensibly vast sums of money were earned.

A film documentary, *That's the Way It Is*, was produced in 1970 and reveals exactly what it was like to be Elvis at this point—and how exhausting playing that role could be. He toured the country that year, making the most of his newfound popularity, revisiting along the way many of the Southern states where he had first become known, 15 years before.

A high point in Elvis' career, and indeed in American sociopolitical history, took place when he met President Richard Nixon at the White House on December

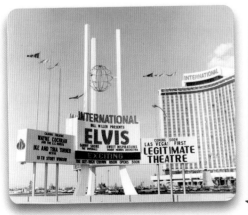

FAR LEFT Seventies Elvis and Las Vegas became hard to separate.

LEFT Meeting Nixon, where Elvis is said to have offered to fix the hippies.

ABOVE Elvis after being presented with a sheriff's badge in 1970.

RIGHT Priscilla and Mike Stone after she divorced Elvis in 1973.

"THE AMERICAN POWER BASE HAD FINALLY COME AROUND TO ELVIS, ALTHOUGH IT WAS TOO LATE TO SAVE HIM.

21, 1970. Accounts of the meeting reveal that Elvis is said to have told Nixon that he could persuade "the hippies" to move away from drugs, and that groups such as The Beatles represented anti-Americanism.

After this, the establishment showed its approval of Elvis, with the Junior Chamber of Commerce naming him one of its annual Ten Most Outstanding Young Men of the Nation, and the City of Memphis named

a stretch of Highway 51 near Graceland as "Elvis Presley Boulevard." In 1971, Elvis was awarded the Lifetime Achievement Award at the Grammys. Another concert film, *Elvis on Tour*, won the Golden Globe Award for Best Documentary Film the following year, while more Grammys and sold-out tours followed. The American power base had finally come around to Elvis, although it was too late to save him.

Despite all this commercial success and industry adulation, Elvis' personal life was starting to become unraveled by 1972. Priscilla Presley divorced him, taking their daughter Lisa Marie and moving in with Elvis' former karate instructor, Mike Stone, an emotional blow from which he is thought never to have recovered. Although a charity concert in January 1973 called *Aloha from Hawaii* was a major success, smashing

BELOW
Advertising the groundbreaking Hawaii concert.

RIGHT
Dr. Nichopoulos confirming the death of Elvis.

FAR RIGHT
After the divorce in 1973, Elvis began to decline.

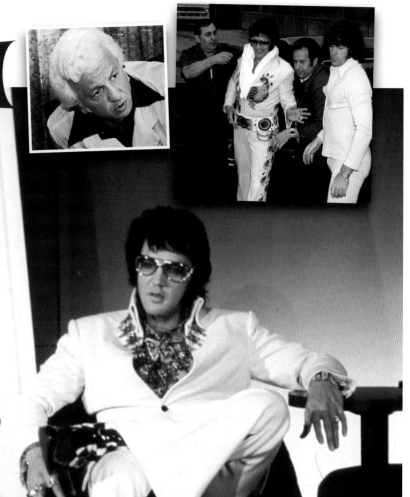

ELVIS
in concert
WORLD WIDE
ALOHA FROM
HAWAII
VIA SATELITE!
JAN. 14, 1973
Presented by RCA RECORD TOURS

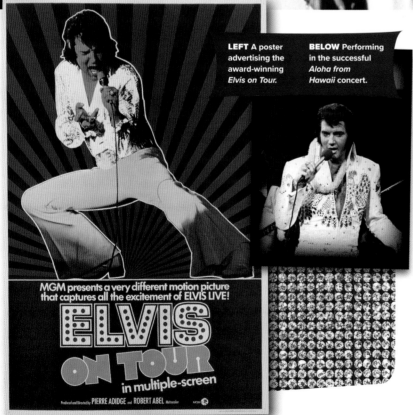

LEFT A poster advertising the award-winning *Elvis on Tour.*

BELOW Performing in the successful *Aloha from Hawaii* concert.

MGM presents a very different motion picture that captures all the excitement of ELVIS LIVE!
ELVIS
ON TOUR
in multiple-screen
Produced and Directed by PIERRE ADIDGE and ROBERT ABEL. Metrocolor

records worldwide, behind the scenes Elvis was developing a serious addiction to uppers and downers prescribed by his personal doctor, George Nichopoulos, although he publicly and privately denied this because he viewed drug addicts as people who injected illegal substances.

When his drug use was added to the consequences of a lifelong diet that was high in fat and low in nutrients, it's obvious why Elvis' physical health began to suffer. His mental health, shaken by Priscilla's departure and exhausted by his punishing schedule, the great man was rapidly becoming a shadow of his former self, and by 1974, audiences and critics were beginning to take notice.

As his guitarist John Wilkinson said, "He was all gut. He was slurring . . . It was obvious he was drugged. It was obvious there was something terribly wrong with his body. It was so bad that the words to the songs were barely intelligible . . . He could barely get through the introductions."

ELVIS COUNTRY
(I'M 10,000 YEARS OLD)

Released **January 1971**

In a burst of inspiration, the 35-year-old Elvis embraces his final peak of creativity.

LEFT This album is somewhat removed from Elvis' problems.

ABOVE Elvis and Priscilla with Welsh singer Tom Jones.

BELOW New tensions had began to arise in Elvis' shows.

TRACKLIST

SIDE ONE

1 Snowbird
2 Tomorrow Never Comes
3 Little Cabin on the Hill
4 Whole Lotta Shakin' Goin' On
5 Funny How Time Slips Away
6 I Really Don't Want to Know

SIDE TWO

1 There Goes My Everything
2 It's Your Baby, You Rock It
3 The Fool
4 Faded Love
5 I Washed My Hands in Muddy Water
6 Make the World Go Away

By 1971, Elvis' lamentably brief comeback, kickstarted by the *'68 Comeback Special*, was on the wane. Prescription drugs and the impending failure of his marriage to Priscilla combined to give his recordings and performances a slight edge of desperation—but in the case of *Elvis Country (I'm 10,000 Years Old)*, this was actually to the benefit of the music.

There are fans who regard *Elvis Country* as his very best album, and it's easy to see why. Recorded in a five-day burst of inspiration with a new producer, Felton Jarvis, and a crack Nashville-based studio band, the songs are passionate, humorous, and yes, slightly aggressive; you can hear Elvis working out his issues.

Start with bluegrass artist Bill Monroe's "Little Cabin on the Hill" and Willie Nelson's "Funny How Time Slips Away," and then work

your way through the tear-jerking "Tomorrow Never Comes." Admire the linking device of "I Was Born About Ten Thousand Years Ago" that makes the reissue LP a sort-of concept album, and take in the fragile "Snowbird," a hit by Anne Murray. Then go straight for a monster version of Jerry Lee Lewis, "Whole Lotta Shakin' Goin' On," perhaps the last true rock 'n' roll studio recording that Elvis ever committed to vinyl.

Honorable mentions must go to guitarist James Burton, who anchored so much of Elvis' later work, and to Jarvis, whose decisions to use songs recorded in one or two takes—and to include studio chatter in the final mix—add great vitality to the album. There's none of the bored, phoning-it-in apathy that Elvis was known for in his final years: instead, this is the sound of a great singer who knows that he stands at the brink of a decline, and sees no reason to accept his fate before it's absolutely necessary.

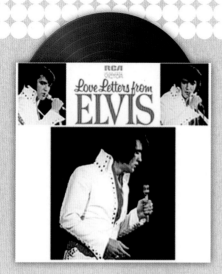

LOVE LETTERS FROM ELVIS

Released June 1971

Not so much a love letter: more of a final demand for a long-overdue bill.

The five-day recording marathon that Elvis burned through in Memphis in 1970 has gone down in Presley legend; seek out the huge 50th-anniversary box set of the sessions from 2020 if you want to get inside the great man's mind at the time. What you don't necessarily want to do is seek out the *Love Letters From Elvis* album, which contains some of those songs—the lesser ones, unfortunately.

It's not all bad, of course: very little that Elvis ever did was truly beyond redemption. The title cut is interesting, with our man on excellent vocal form, even if the backing musicians don't know if they're supposed to be playing funk or easy listening. "Got My Mojo Working" is over the top but compelling in its way, even though it too sits uneasily on a seventies Elvis album. Then there's "Cindy, Cindy" which has plenty of energy, if not a whole lot else to recommend it.

Sadly, that's more or less it for the *Love Letters* LP. By this point in his career, Elvis should really have been addressing more serious subjects than affairs of the heart, and his fans knew it. What's most aggravating about this half-listenable record is that it puts a full stop to the renewed flow of creativity that had begun after the *'68 Special*, when there was no real need for it to dry up just yet. Elvis was on the brink of revitalized greatness, we had all been led to think—we just hadn't realized that his return to the top would be so brief.

Rolling Stone magazine summarized the point best: "Those of us who have loved him from the beginning, and know that he could still be doing it, because every now and then we can still hear him doing it, can only turn away in disgust from this sort of thing."

BELOW Elvis still serenading fans at his live shows in 1971.

MIDDLE A slightly less jovial Elvis after a lunch in his honor.

BOTTOM It wasn't all gloom— Elvis joking with press.

TRACKLIST

SIDE ONE
1 Love Letters
2 When I'm Over You
3 If I Were You
4 Got My Mojo Working
5 Heart of Rome

SIDE TWO
1 Only Believe
2 This Is Our Dance
3 Cindy, Cindy
4 I'll Never Know
5 It Ain't No Big Thing (But It's Growing)
6 Life

Images Elvis Presley (album covers), Getty Images, Alamy

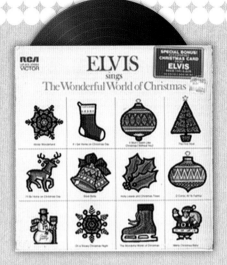

ELVIS SINGS THE WONDERFUL WORLD OF CHRISTMAS

Released **October 1971**

It's round two for Santa Elvis and his merry Yuletide cover versions.

Elvis Presley's Christmas album of 1957 did well because he was a hot young rebel at the time, making it a curio, and because life was more innocent back then. In the late fifties, you could slip the LP on, sip a martini, and be happy that World War II was receding rapidly into history. By the time Elvis released 1971's *Elvis Sings The Wonderful World of Christmas*, he was a middle-aged dad and the Vietnam war was underway.

Still, who doesn't like to slip into an eggnog-fueled trance and ignore the outside world for a bit while listening to "O Come, All Ye Faithful"? You certainly have to give it to Elvis and his handlers—when they wanted to indulge in a bit of Yuletide sentimentality, they chose exactly the right songs. Elvis sang them beautifully, too, overlaying the soulful, sometimes countrified tunes with a well-gauged performance.

Some of the material is predictable, if also enjoyable—see "The First Noel"—but there are some mild surprises, too. Elvis upped the tempo of "Silver Bells" for some added oomph, while a new backing troupe called the Imperials shone on "The Wonderful World of Christmas." He shows off his still-wondrous vocal chops on "It Won't Seem Like Christmas" and beefs up "Winter Wonderland" to the status of rocker. There are two moderately bluesy workouts to enjoy in "I'll Be Home on Christmas Day" and "Merry Christmas Baby," too.

Credit must go to the fabulous backing musicians who made the session work so well, among them guitarist James Burton and bassist Norbert Putnam. Together, Elvis and band pulled it off: the question was really whether we needed a second chunk of seasonal Presley in the first place.

TRACKLIST

SIDE ONE

1 **O Come, All Ye Faithful**
2 **The First Noel**
3 **On a Snowy Christmas Night**
4 **Winter Wonderland**
5 **The Wonderful World of Christmas**
6 **It Won't Seem Like Christmas (Without You)**

SIDE TWO

1 **I'll Be Home on Christmas Day**
2 **If I Get Home on Christmas Day**
3 **Holly Leaves and Christmas Trees**
4 **Merry Christmas Baby**
5 **Silver Bells**
6 **Blue Christmas**

FAR LEFT Surely this is how a rock 'n' roll Santa would look?

LEFT Possibly the best Christmas card ever designed.

RIGHT Another glorious Christmas card of Elvis and Colonel Tom.

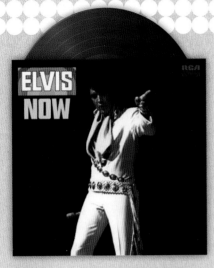

ELVIS NOW

Released **February 1972**

With a less throwaway title and concept, this LP would have been much better. As it is, *Elvis Now* is a mixed bag.

Elvis Now doesn't exactly make much of an effort to impress the listener. As a random collection of unrelated songs, it doesn't really have a central theme to grab onto, and its title and artwork don't help—reinforcing the accusation by many critics that Elvis was a great singer, but he never made a coherent album.

Cobbled together from songs recorded in January 1969, the Nashville sessions of 1970, and others in May and June of 1971, the album is a mixture of spirituals, covers of contemporary pop hits, and a few tracks that are best described as "Elvis in the seventies." It's all very Las Vegas in the arrangements and delivery, with big swooshing dynamics rising and falling as Elvis emotes, which made sense because Vegas was very much his chosen spiritual home at this point.

On the plus side, Elvis did a decent job of interpreting at least four major hits by other artists. Of these, the best known is The Beatles' "Hey Jude," and the Presley version is both subtler and better than you might think. The next best song on the album is probably George Hamilton IV's plaintive 1966 hit "Early Morning Rain," written by the Canadian singer Gordon Lightfoot and also covered by Bob Dylan. Here, Elvis takes an admirable stab at the song, leading off with some studio chat and delivering a surprisingly tender rendition.

The most dedicated Presley disciples will be fascinated by "I Was Born About Ten Thousand Years Ago," in which the occult scholar reveals his religious inspirations. "I'll lick the guy that says it isn't so!" he warns, on a piece of music that is both upbeat and fascinating, unlike much of the filler material here.

TRACKLIST

SIDE ONE

1 Help Me Make it through the Night
2 Miracle of the Rosary
3 Hey Jude
4 Put Your Hand in the Hand
5 Until It's Time for You to Go

SIDE TWO

1 We Can Make the Morning
2 Early Mornin' Rain
3 Sylvia
4 Fools Rush In (Where Angels Fear to Tread)
5 I Was Born About Ten Thousand Years Ago

TOP Sequins and cape can only mean one thing— seventies Elvis!

ABOVE Elvis before his Madison Square Garden concert.

RIGHT Belting out another tune while on a concert tour.

Images Elvis Presley (album covers), Getty Images, Alamy

89

HE TOUCHED ME

Released April 1972

Gospel album number three is a surprisingly decent, modern-sounding record.

Elvis doesn't repeat the formula of *His Hand In Mine* and *How Great Thou Art* on *He Touched Me*—not an album title that would be used in the more cynical modern era, we can safely predict. The "Christian rock" sound in this album isn't for everyone, least of all for fans of his golden rock 'n' roll period, but *He Touched Me* is definitely moving forward.

Essentially, Elvis has landed on a contemporary gospel sound here, "contemporary" meaning that a full electric band accompanies the vocals. The Imperials and JD Sumner & The Stamps supply excellent backing vocals, and the arrangements leave enough space for the music to breathe. There's much less of the overstuffed, Las Vegas-style instrumentation that had plagued some

of his recent albums, which is welcome because it allows Elvis space for vocal nuances.

There are traditional gospel songs here, such as "Bosom of Abraham" and "I, John," both of which do the trick reasonably well, but the real gold lies in songs by Dallas Frazier ("He Is My Everything"), Andraé Crouch ("I've Got Confidence"), and Bill Gaither's title cut. There are the expected lonesome ballads, "Reach Out to Jesus" among them, and a version of "Amazing Grace" on which Elvis stretches out without being schmaltzy. There's even a rocker, "I've Got Confidence," and a Red West-penned contribution in the form of "Seeing is Believing." In spite of everything, it seemed that Elvis still had what it took: if only he'd been given more time to use his talents.

TRACKLIST

SIDE ONE
1 He Touched Me
2 I've Got Confidence
3 Amazing Grace
4 Seeing Is Believing
5 He Is My Everything
6 Bosom of Abraham

SIDE TWO
1 An Evening Prayer
2 Lead Me, Guide Me
3 There Is No God but God
4 A Thing Called Love
5 I, John
6 Reach Out to Jesus

FAR LEFT Elvis recording an arrangement in 1972.

LEFT A still from *Elvis on Tour*, a film that was released in 1972.

ABOVE No matter what happened, religion was part of Elvis' life.

ELVIS (FOOL)

Released **July 1973**

Strip away the extraneous music, give Elvis a piano, and watch his unique genius unfold.

ABOVE Elvis being warmly greeted in Hawaii, 1973.

RIGHT Performing to a gleeful audience in Honolulu, Hawaii in January, 1973.

R eferred to as *Elvis (Fool)* or *The Fool Album* to avoid confusion with Elvis' first two albums, and indeed the plethora of Presley releases which bore his first name somewhere in their title, this mononymous LP has a single saving grace. This is that three of the songs are just Elvis and a piano, the instrument which had become his best vehicle as his career ebbed. Remember how we talked about his impromptu live rendition of the Righteous Brothers' "Unchained Melody"? These songs are less dramatic, but just as spine-tinglingly effective.

The solo tracks aside—"It's Still Here," "I'll Take You Home Again, Kathleen," and "I Will Be True"—this LP is a grab bag of outtakes, recorded at sessions in Nashville in March 1971 and May 1972. There's also a live version of "It's Impossible," recorded at one of the Vegas gigs. Be advised that the word "outtakes" doesn't mean that the music is not worth your time: students of Presley psychology will love the studio banter and commentary, especially if they invest in the double-CD version that first came out in 1994.

Elsewhere, we're given a harmonica-laden take on Paul Williams' "Where Do I Go From Here" and a jam through Bob Dylan's "Don't Think Twice, It's All Right": a much longer version of the latter exists, so track it down if this three-minute edit doesn't hit the spot. Here, the Taking Care Of Business band really show their worth, backing the maestro with understanding and skill. There are some songs that miss the mark—"Padre" is one of them, with Elvis emoting way too much—but they didn't stop the LP from selling reasonably well.

TRACKLIST

SIDE ONE

1 Fool
2 Where Do I Go from Here?
3 Love Me, Love the Life I Lead
4 It's Still Here
5 It's Impossible

SIDE TWO

1 (That's What You Get) For Lovin' Me
2 Padre
3 I'll Take You Home Again, Kathleen
4 I Will Be True
5 Don't Think Twice, It's All Right

CHAPTER 3
....
Inside GRACELAND

DISCOGRAPHY

LIFE
with *Elvis*

What was it like to be a friend, relative, or wife of the biggest star in the world?

RIGHT Elvis and Priscilla in happier times—on their wedding day in 1967.

I f you think it was hard to be Elvis Presley, being married to him would have been just as bad—or even worse. At least Elvis only battled his own demons. His wife Priscilla, to whom he was married for six years, had to deal with him, his friends, his fans, and swarms of yes-people who constantly wanted a piece of him, all the while trying to raise their daughter in a situation that was surreal at best and downright terrifying at worst.

Ten years younger than her husband, Priscilla Presley—or Priscilla Beaulieu, as she was when they first met in 1959—was destined to find the marriage difficult from the start. A hip kid in the sixties when Elvis was in early middle age, the daughter of military privilege while he was raised

LEFT A copy of Elvis and Priscilla's marriage certificate.

MIDDLE LEFT The couple stressed their relationship was platonic at the beginning.

TOP LEFT Performing their vows at the Aladdin Hotel in Las Vegas.

ABOVE Cutting the very impressive wedding cake.

in extreme poverty, she was completely different from him in almost every way. Furthermore, he was famous and she was not, and when they met, she was a child and he an adult.

Somehow, the relationship worked, at least for a few years. Their very early friendship was dogged by endless speculation in the press as to whether they were sleeping together—which, then as now, would have been illegal given her youth. Priscilla maintained that the relationship remained platonic until she was of age, and indeed that it remained unconsummated until their wedding day, at Elvis' insistence.

This was the kind of public speculation that surrounded the relationship of Elvis and Priscilla—an intrusion that would have doomed many marriages. Still, the pressure was on for the union to take place, not least from manager Colonel Tom, who reminded Elvis that a so-called "morality clause" formed part of his contract with RCA. Once the couple became husband and wife on May 1, 1967, in a quick ceremony in—where else?—Las Vegas, Priscilla became pregnant, giving birth to their daughter Lisa Marie Presley nine months to the day later.

The 32-year-old Elvis was now a family man, inasmuch as he could be given his professional schedule, and reports from Priscilla and others indicate that the early days of their marriage were happy ones. He bought her a horse named Domino as a Christmas present, the first in a Graceland stable that continues to this day, and the couple spent time together whenever they could. Unfortunately, the specter of infidelity soon loomed over their marriage: as early as 1968, Priscilla found herself briefly involved with a dance instructor who she identified only as Mark. "I needed more out of my relationship with Elvis," she later wrote. At only 23 years old, and constantly apart from her husband, she must have found aspects of her life with him deeply unsatisfying.

For his part, Elvis is also thought to have had illicit affairs with the co-stars of the movies he was making. It's difficult to

" **ELVIS WAS NOW A FAMILY MAN, INASMUCH AS HE COULD BE GIVEN HIS SCHEDULE, AND REPORTS FROM PRISCILLA AND OTHERS INDICATE THE EARLY DAYS OF THEIR MARRIAGE WERE HAPPY ONES.**

TOP LEFT Elvis at home with one of his horses—ever the years he built up stables.

TOP RIGHT A very young Priscilla Beaulieu posing while playing an Elvis record.

ABOVE The proud parents photographed with four-day-old Lisa Marie.

LEFT Despite a happy start, the Presley marriage soon began to crack.

MIDDLE Elvis and Priscilla holding hands after their divorce hearing in October 1973.

RIGHT Priscilla and Elvis' karate instructor, Mike Stone, who she moved in with.

LEFT Priscilla, Elvis, and Lisa Marie enjoying some family time in Hawaii.

BELOW Elvis tasked his parents with finding a home they could all live in.

" ELVIS IS ALSO THOUGHT TO HAVE HAD ILLICIT AFFAIRS WITH THE CO-STARS OF THE MOVIES HE WAS MAKING.

know exactly with whom and when these dalliances occurred because accounts vary wildly, but he is thought to have been in a sporadic relationship with a Capitol Hill member of staff called Joyce Bova from 1969 to 1972. Bova even claimed that she became pregnant by Elvis and underwent an abortion, and while these details were not made public at the time, the endless rumors and denials were evidently enough to drive the Presleys apart. If you believe the scurrilous Albert Goldman biography *Elvis* (1981), then the singer's personal habits—including poor hygiene and a strange relationship with food—also played a part in their estrangement.

Most of all, though, Priscilla had the giant, flawed personality of Elvis Presley to deal with. Living with a man who had never really matured from boyhood, who gained self-esteem from a flock of hangers-on, and whose psyche had been damaged beyond repair by the premature death of his mother, would have been close to impossible—even if he hadn't been the most famous man in the world.

The end came when Priscilla embarked on a serious affair with Mike Stone, Elvis' former karate instructor. Ironically, it was Elvis who had introduced the two, suggesting that she take up the martial art to pass the time. "Elvis must have perceived my new restlessness," she later wrote, adding that the affair led her to end the marriage. They separated on February 23, 1972, with the divorce finalized a year and a half later. After some negotiation, Priscilla was awarded $725,000—around $5 million today—plus other allowances.

Elvis was deeply hurt by the end of his marriage, at one point expressing furious hatred towards Stone. "There's too much pain in me . . . Stone must die," he fumed, leading his friend Red West to inquire about a contract killing. Fortunately for all involved, Elvis calmed down, muttering "Aw hell, let's just leave it for now. Maybe it's a bit heavy."

This leads us to the infamous Memphis Mafia, the group of men who orbited Elvis at his invitation from his early fame through to his death in 1977. These were in many ways the closest relationships he had, with no mother or sibling to occupy an equal family status, and only an ineffectual father, Vernon, who was reduced to the level of business manager. It's obvious that Elvis sought a sense of brotherhood from these men—in fact, it has been theorized that this came from a longing for his stillborn twin, Jesse—but true camaraderie always eluded him. You can't be truly friends with people who you pay to stick around, and who do so solely for that reason.

On the subject of money, it emerged some years after Elvis' death that the members of his entourage were not paid large sums, usually no more than $500 a week—this was a decent salary in 1970, but no more than that. Instead, Elvis' reputation for generosity was based on his fondness for buying lavish gifts for his so-called friends. These often included cars and expensive jewelry, but would even extend as far as houses on occasion. The members of the Mafia would be fulsome in their gratitude, as well as possessive of their relationship with their high-earning master—it's unlikely, in those unenlightened days, that any of them stopped to reflect that what Elvis was actually buying with these ridiculous gifts was their loyalty and their silence.

Yes, perhaps that analysis is a little harsh. In reality, there was genuine friendship between many of the Mafia and their boss. Some of them were related to him, and others were friends from childhood, so that mutual bond was real. The first core members of the group were Elvis' cousins Junior and Gene Smith, his high school friend Red

WINNING ISN'T IMPO...

ABOVE Elvis and some of his Memphis Mafia, a group of friends (albeit paid) who helped give a sense of kinship to the star.

West, and a singer named Cliff Gleaves. They were soon joined by Judy Spreckels, the only woman to have been a part of the gang. She later explained, "There wasn't a crowd then, just a few guys... [I] had nothing to do with being a yes-man for him, and obviously he trusted me."

Of these, Red West is probably the best known, as he helped write music for Elvis and later enjoyed a brief career as an actor in films such as *Road House* (1989). His cousin Sonny West also later joined the Memphis Mafia. Other well-known names were Charlie Hodge, Joe Esposito, Alan Fortas, Marty Lacker, Jerry Schilling, and Lamar Fike, although many other men played lesser roles over the years.

The public perception of this bunch of buddies varied. Initially they were looked upon favorably, as a gang of friendly

LEFT Linda Thompson had a four-year relationship with Elvis.

RIGHT Elvis and high school friend Red West, who was part of the Memphis Mafia.

" THE WASN'T A CROWD THEN, JUST A FEW GUYS... [I] HAD NOTHING TO DO WITH BEING A YES-MAN FOR HIM.

 Judy Spreckels

Images Getty Images, Alamy

RIGHT Elvis and his cousin, Gene Smith, a core member of the Memphis Mafia.

BELOW Judy Spreckels was an early member of the Mafia and the only woman.

BOTTOM Ginger Alden was Elvis' last relationship and the last one to see him alive.

chums who liked to horse around so that the overworked Elvis could have some fun in his downtime. Most of them did perform useful work for the Presley industry, as Lacker put it, "Everyone had assigned responsibilities and they were far from leeches, hangers-on, or whatever else they were called . . . as far as being there for the money, that's laughable because there really wasn't much in that area to be there for . . . we were there because we all cared about Elvis and each other like brothers."

The Mafia were particularly useful on tour with Elvis, where Esposito handled the money and travel arrangements, Hodge played guitar in the band, Fike was on stage lights, Schilling dispensed audio advice, and the two West cousins were on security detail. Life on the road was a lot of fun, said Esposito: "It was a party like you wouldn't believe. Go to a different show every night, then pick up a bunch of women afterwards, go party the next night. Go to the lounges, see Fats Domino, Della Reese, Jackie Wilson, The Four Aces, The Dominoes—all the old acts. We'd stay there and never sleep, we were all taking pills just so we could keep up with each other."

And so the good times rolled. As for Elvis' romantic relationships, post-Priscilla, aside from supposed one-offs with groupies—according to Albert Goldman, there seems to have been little of note. He did have a four-year arrangement with a former Memphis beauty queen named Linda Thompson from 1972 to 1976, and his final relationship from late that year until his death was with an actress, Ginger Alden. By then he was in poor shape, physically and mentally, and incapable of giving either what they wanted—a normal life.

Normality was always out of Elvis' reach, though, because his relationships were permanently twisted by fame and dysfunction. If there's a price to be paid for wealth and adulation, then that's it, right there.

A HOME Fit for a KING

Whether you prefer tack or taste, Graceland is the most famous rock star home in the world. Let's take a peek inside . . .

Touch down at Memphis International Airport, drive west, and take Elvis Presley Boulevard southbound for around six minutes. You'll find yourself approaching a hill, surrounded by pastures, on top of which is a two-story building that fans of the late King will instantly recognize.

Even if you've never heard of Graceland, the legendary country home where Elvis lived from March 1957 until he died there, 20 years and five months later, you'll learn its name as your car rolls along the Boulevard. Everywhere you look, there is a forest of signs proclaiming the attractions of dozens of ancillary businesses boasting the name Elvis or those of his parents. Graceland Chapel in the Woods is over here. Graceland RV Park is over there. Vernon's Smokehouse is around the corner . . .

The story of Graceland is, in many ways, the story of its famous owner, although it was just another country mansion for many years before Elvis moved in. Built in 1939 as part of a 500-acre farm belonging to the Toof family, Graceland was named after a relative and occupied by her descendants until it went on the market in the mid-fifties. The design was in the Colonial Revival style, covered in stucco and Mississippi limestone. Touches of opulence, such as columns at the corners of the portico,

Images Getty Images, Alamy

ABOVE Graceland was one of the very few constants in Elvis' life.

LEFT Actress Yvonne Lime with Elvis while visiting him for a weekend in 1957.

stained-glass windows, a balcony, and stone steps flanked by lions make it clear that this is no starter home.

That said, it nearly was for Elvis. He'd bought his first property already—a wholly acceptable town house at 1034 Audubon Drive in Memphis—for $40,000. This alone was a feat of social climbing that would have been literally inconceivable back in his childhood shack in Tupelo. The neighbors soon got sick of the endless crowds around the house, though, and just a year or two after his first flush of fame, Elvis realized that something rather more ambitious was going to be needed.

This was where Gladys and Vernon came in. In early 1957, Elvis told them that he had set aside $100,000 for them to find a suitable house for them all to live in. Although they were unlikely to have had much experience in house-hunting at this level—their budget was equivalent to over a million dollars in today's money—the proud parents had an idea, suggesting Graceland as a possible acquisition. Elvis duly shelled out $102,500, presumably not finding it too hard to come up with the extra two-and-a-half grand, and the Presleys moved in.

> ## HE WASTED NO TIME IN MAKING IT FIT FOR HIMSELF, HIS BUDDIES, AND HIS GIRLFRIENDS, IN A RIOT OF COLOR.

Gladys was unable to enjoy her new home for long, dying of heart failure in 1958, and indeed Elvis himself was rarely there until 1960, thanks to his military service overseas. Once installed, though, he wasted no time in making it fit for himself, his buddies, and his girlfriends, in a riot of color and ornamentation that could be described as "extravagant" at best and "deranged" at worst.

In fairness to the young millionaire, he did have 17,552 square feet and 23 rooms to decorate. The key rooms at Graceland are well known for their relentless opulence, including a living room with a 15-foot-long white sofa and white

TOP The infamous musical note front gate of Graceland.

MIDDLE Stained-glass peacocks in an otherwise stark living room.

ABOVE A personalized glass panel above the front door.

LEFT The Jungle Room, a riot of wood and green tropical fun.

fireplace that was accessed through a classical, ellipse-shaped entryway; a music room with a black baby grand piano and a doorway framed by peacocks set in stained glass; a dining room with rounded curio cabinets and black marble flooring; and Vernon and Gladys' bedroom, tricked out in tasteful purple, white, and pink.

The most fun was had elsewhere, though— and at 22 years old, the nominally single, insanely wealthy Elvis and his buddies were determined to party like there was no tomorrow. One of his first moves was to extend the house to include the "Jungle Room." It famously included an indoor waterfall and was eventually converted into a recording studio for Elvis' last two albums, *From Elvis Presley Boulevard, Memphis, Tennessee* (1976) and *Moody Blue* (1977). He also added a wing on the south side of the main house that connected the music room to the swimming pool, a massive slot-car racing track, and a basement TV room and bar. Here he often watched three televisions at once or listened to a state-of-the-art stereo system, while a billiards room was nearby.

Still, Elvis was just getting started, eventually

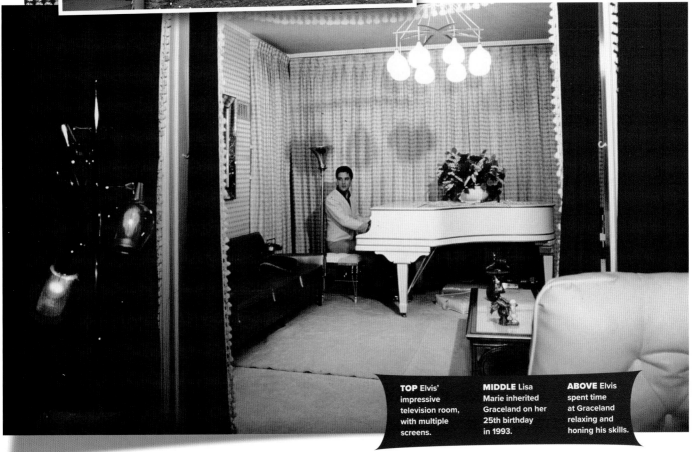

TOP Elvis' impressive television room, with multiple screens.

MIDDLE Lisa Marie inherited Graceland on her 25th birthday in 1993.

ABOVE Elvis spent time at Graceland relaxing and honing his skills.

ABOVE The pool room, with a spectacular ceiling.

ABOVE A visitor to Graceland takes in an impressive wall of memorabilia.

BELOW Elvis on his 15-foot white sofa in the living room.

BOTTOM Elvis having some fun on three-wheelers at Graceland in 1975.

> " ELVIS LOVED GRACELAND . . . HE IS SAID TO HAVE HAD HIS HOTEL ROOMS REARRANGED WHILE ON TOUR SO THAT THEY RESEMBLED [IT].

spending over half a million dollars on remodeling the former farm mansion. For security, he built a pink Alabama fieldstone wall on the perimeter, which was soon covered in graffiti; he installed a kidney shaped swimming pool; and added a wrought-iron front gate covered in green musical notes. He then installed a racquetball court in the style of a traditional country club, dressed in dark leather and featuring a sunken seating area; this came with a shatterproof floor-to-ceiling window so that guests could spectate while games were going on.

Later in life, as Elvis became fixated on spiritual matters, he asked the architect Bernard Grenadier to design and build a Meditation Garden; he used this area to reflect on his problems. Did he know that he would eventually be buried there? Perhaps, as his stillborn twin brother Jesse was memorialized there, his mother Gladys was buried there, and eventually his father and grandmother Minnie Mae Hood Presley ended up there, too.

Elsewhere on the Graceland estate,

Elvis installed an office for his father, the aforementioned smokehouse where he stored an arsenal of weapons, and a stable for his many horses. Other areas of the property have never been accessible to the public, however, in particular Elvis' bedroom at the southwest corner, his office, and his daughter

Lisa Marie's bedroom in the northeast corner. The bathroom where he died has remained private, with the owners knowing full well that this room would otherwise attract much attention, and many of the living, dining, and cooking quarters were occupied as recently as 1993 by Elvis' aunt Delta, who lived there after the rest of the Presley family had died or moved away.

Graceland, and by implication Elvis himself, are often mocked for the tastelessness of the decor, but ask yourself two questions. One, did your house look ridiculous in the seventies by today's standards? Two, would you go overboard with the furnishings if you moved from abject poverty to oligarch-style wealth in the space of a couple of years? The answer to both questions is likely yes.

In any case, the real point is that Elvis loved Graceland with a passion. He was incredibly proud of it for obvious reasons, once claiming that the US government had considered showing the property to the Soviet Union as a successful example of rags-to-riches capitalism. He also needed the security it gave him, not only physical but also psychological—he is said to have had his hotel rooms rearranged while on tour so that they resembled his Memphis mansion. And why not? In a world as surreal as his, any symbols of familiarity and safety would have been welcome, even essential.

Visit Graceland if you can. More than just a tourist stop, the building is the closest we will ever get to seeing inside the mind of Elvis Presley. That is its true, ongoing value.

Images Getty Images, Alamy

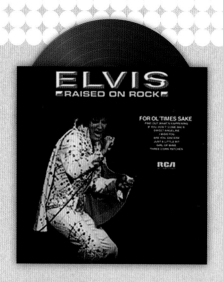

RAISED ON ROCK / FOR OL' TIMES SAKE

Released **October 1973**

The good times were gone and the sad times were here ... but there were glimmers of hope.

LEFT Elvis performing in 1973, along with a trusty towel.

ABOVE The sadness Elvis felt in 1973 was often noticeable.

RIGHT Elvis in his jumpsuit that set him back a mere $5,000.

TRACKLIST

SIDE ONE

1 Raised on Rock
2 Are You Sincere?
3 Find Out What's Happening
4 I Miss You
5 Girl of Mine

SIDE TWO

1 For Ol' Times Sake
2 If You Don't Come Back
3 Just a Little Bit
4 Sweet Angeline
5 Three Corn Patches

By late 1973, Elvis was unhappy and unwell. His divorce from Priscilla had left him crushed. However, his muse, musically speaking at least, hadn't quite deserted him: he is said to have recorded 18 songs in a single week at a session in December, recorded at the famous Stax Studios with his established band and a few new guys.

Raised on Rock / For Ol' Times Sake has a curious title which only makes sense when you grasp that each phrase refers to the opening track of each side; these were also issued as a single, just to add to the confusion at which the Elvis-era RCA excelled. Some of the new songs are surprisingly enjoyable, especially given that the psychological circumstances in which they were recorded were less than ideal. "Find Out What's

Happening" is probably *Raised on Rock*'s best track, along with a version of Jimmy Reed's "Just A Little Bit" and a fully leaded ballad, "Are You Sincere?"

Whether you enjoy this LP or not will at least partly depend on your tolerance for Elvis' depressed mood. His sadness and vulnerability as his life spirals out of control are almost audible on songs such as Jerry Leiber and Mike Stoller's "If You Don't Come Back," where we hear an emotional interplay between Elvis and his female backing singers. The exact same can be said of "For Ol' Times Sake," practically an appeal to Priscilla to dump the kung fu guy and come home. Like "Always on My Mind" and "Separate Ways," the song reminds us that behind the extroversion, there was a man capable of profound sadness.

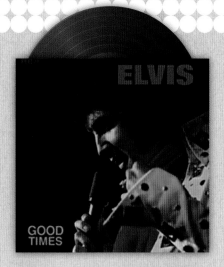

GOOD TIMES

Released **March 1974**

Perhaps *More or Less Adequate Times* would have been a more appropriate title for this collection.

Recorded in the summer and autumn of 1973 at Stax Studios in Memphis, *Good Times* suffers from the same malaise as much of Elvis' early seventies output—in other words, there are a couple of decent songs, and the rest were neither good enough to be engaging nor bad enough to be irritating. He deserved much better, but by now it was clear that he was never going to get it.

There's some energy in the loved-up "I've Got a Thing About You, Baby," even if it doesn't stand up next to the vintage rock 'n' rollers of Elvis' youth—although what song ever could?

Elvis is singing well here, especially when backed up by a thunderous gospel choir on "If That Isn't Love." One of the many ballads, "My Boy," is among the few really enjoyable cuts, although anyone who doesn't like this aspect of Elvis' music will find it deeply cheesy. Such listeners will prefer the amped-up take on Dennis Linde's "I Got a Feelin' in My Body," but even the most hardhearted Presley-watcher will find something to like about softer songs such as "Good Time Charlie's Got the Blues" and "Loving Arms."

Still, it's hard to defend *Good Times*. It's not a terrible album by any means, but there's a lugubrious air of melancholy throughout, which can get a little wearing after a while. Like so many late-in-the-day Presley records, you have to ask yourself if the world really needed this album. What does it achieve, other than slip another hundred grand in the Presley and Parker pockets and remind everyone that Elvis was much better in the old days?

TRACKLIST

SIDE ONE

1 **Take Good Care of Her**
2 **Loving Arms**
3 **I Got a Feelin' in My Body**
4 **If That Isn't Love**
5 **She Wears My Ring**

SIDE TWO

1 **I've Got a Thing About You Baby**
2 **My Boy**
3 **Spanish Eyes**
4 **Talk About the Good Times**
5 **Good Time Charlie's Got the Blues**

LEFT Elvis wearing his signature leather jacket and shades.

MIDDLE Crowds of people would still gather to see Elvis in 1974.

RIGHT On stage during one of his last shows at Niagara Falls.

Images Elvis Presley (album covers), Getty Images, Alamy

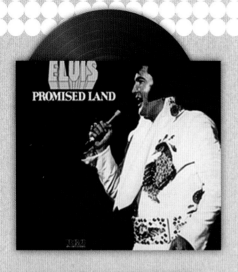

PROMISED LAND

Released **January 1975**

A mixed bag, sure, but there are one or two gems to enjoy in this roundup of Stax-recorded material.

LEFT It's easy to forget Elvis still had his twinkle in later years.

ABOVE It's also easy to forget he still got physical in concert.

BELOW This album proved Elvis could still bring it.

TRACKLIST

SIDE ONE

1 Promised Land
2 There's a Honky Tonk Angel (Who'll Take Me Back In)
3 Help Me
4 Mr. Songman
5 Love Song of the Year

SIDE TWO

1 It's Midnight
2 Your Love's Been a Long Time Coming
3 If You Talk in Your Sleep
4 Thinking About You
5 You Asked Me To

There's a fair amount to enjoy on *Promised Land,* which gathers the previously unreleased songs from the December Stax sessions that made up the *Good Times* album. This LP is slightly better, including a fully realized "It's Midnight," a funked-up "If You Talk in Your Sleep," and the title track. This song, an old Chuck Berry number, takes on renewed life with Elvis' rendition, perhaps because he was in relatively good shape and well rested when he recorded it. He sounds passionate on "It's Midnight," too, which is just as well as these songs demand commitment from any singer: without it, they would sound half-baked.

The rest of it mostly passes muster. There's blues-tinged pop music in "Your Love's Been a Long Time Coming," and some enjoyable interplay livens up "Mr. Songman." Much of the material is lightweight and undemanding rather than the full soul and gospel experience, but that's fine when it comes to "You Asked Me To"

and "Help Me." Of course, this being late-career Elvis, there's lots of filler, with "There's a Honky Tonk Angel" and "Love Song of the Year," both pretty slight, despite the latter's ambitious title.

It's interesting to look at the bigger picture here. *Promised Land* emerged from the last studio sessions that Elvis ever made in Memphis, in a full-circle move that acknowledges his trajectory there and back again. He wasn't completely phoning in his performances, either: there's evident gusto in many of these songs, especially those he covered by master songwriters such as Chuck Berry, Waylon Jennings, and Larry Gatlin.

If the album isn't quite as heartfelt as *Elvis Country* or as soulful as *From Elvis in Memphis,* that's only to be expected given the circumstances. Had any form of quality control been exercised by his management, we would have been treated to one or two excellent albums instead of three mostly good ones, but hindsight is definitely 20/20 in this regard.

TODAY

Released **May 1975**

A decent final studio album by any standards, with some interesting song choices from the master.

Between March 10 and 12, 1975, Elvis recorded his final studio sessions at RCA's Studio C in Los Angeles. There's no audible clue in his performances that he was about to enter a physical decline: in fact, on *Today* he sounds fresh, enthusiastic, and in full command of the material. It's bittersweet to hear this, as this LP was the last non-live, non-compilation album released in his lifetime.

Sure, the production is bland and unchallenging, but you wouldn't be listening to this LP expecting to hear a Fairlight sampler and pan pipes anyway. Many of the songs check all the boxes, from a beefed-up run-through of "T-R-O-U-B-L-E" as the opening cut, to Don McLean's heartfelt "And I Love You So." Billy Swan's "I Can Help" is propelled by a real earworm, a guitar line that repeats relentlessly, and has an unusual but interesting sentiment in the line, "Let me help, if your child needs a daddy, I can help.

It would sure do me good to do you good, let me help."

There's some downhome country and western in "Susan When She Tried," leading the listener to consider the vocal similarities between Elvis and Johnny Cash, and then there's a splendid rendition of Tom Jones's "Green, Green Grass of Home." The Welsh wonder had an odd relationship with the older American, outsinging his mentor while enjoying a real friendship with him, so who knows what this song represents. Elvis' attempt to remind the young pretender who was boss, perhaps?

If you're still struggling with the fact that Elvis died in 1977, just two years after this LP was released, you're not alone. We all shake our heads in bemusement at this simple, shocking fact, even 45 years later. Listening to this energetic, if flawed, album doesn't help. How could a singer as vigorous as this, aged just 40, be so close to self-destruction?

TRACKLIST

SIDE ONE

1 T-R-O-U-B-L-E
2 And I Love You So
3 Susan When She Tried
4 Woman Without Love
5 Shake a Hand

SIDE TWO

1 Pieces of My Life
2 Fairytale
3 I Can Help
4 Bringing It Back
5 Green, Green Grass of Home

FAR LEFT Elvis could command an audience whatever stage of career he was at.

LEFT When this was taken, Elvis had just over 19 months to live.

BELOW left Still bringing the Elvis magic to Las Vegas in December 1975.

RIGHT This album was the last one Elvis would record in a studio.

FROM ELVIS PRESLEY BOULEVARD, MEMPHIS, TENNESSEE

Released May 1976

**The sound of a singer accepting his fate...
or just a few lo-fi home recordings?**

By 1976, Elvis was done with studios and chose to record this curious LP at Graceland, partly in front of an invited audience. This explains the "Recorded Live" claim on the album's cover, although its cheery image of the great man commanding the stage doesn't reflect the nature of the material in the grooves.

Mostly melancholic and over-blessed with sad or reflective songs, this LP won't make most listeners happy. It's not that Elvis can't sing the songs well, but the production is a little unnerving because the engineers recording at Graceland attempted to mask the limitations of the non-studio environment. This entailed adding far too much extraneous stuff, whether that meant layers of strings or far too many backing vocals. Stripped down, the songs would have been more effective, and who cares if they sound like they're recorded in his living room?

Despite the tweaking, there are some memorable songs here, just as there are on every Elvis LP. "Hurt" is one of the best songs he ever recorded, and if the traditional "Danny Boy" is a bit miserable, at least Elvis pulls off some impressive falsetto acrobatics. "Solitaire" and the passionate "I'll Never Fall in Love Again" make being gloomy sound at least a bit interesting, and there's a dash of upbeat rock in "For the Heart." Even "The Last Farewell," an unusual song choice, keeps the listener engaged just because it's not the usual Presley fare.

You could interpret this album as the sound of Elvis accepting his age and wondering what the future held, and anyone who has recently turned 40—or is about to do so—will understand this frame of mind.

TRACKLIST

SIDE ONE
1 Hurt
2 Never Again
3 Blue Eyes Crying in the Rain
4 Danny Boy
5 The Last Farewell

SIDE TWO
1 For the Heart
2 Bitter They Are, Harder They Fall
3 Solitaire
4 Love Coming Down
5 I'll Never Fall in Love Again

ABOVE LEFT The 1976 Elvis didn't quite look like the Elvis on the LP.

LEFT Elvis in what was his last Memphis show, July 5, 1976.

ABOVE Entering his private plane—the Lisa Marie—bought in 1976.

MOODY BLUE

Released July 1977

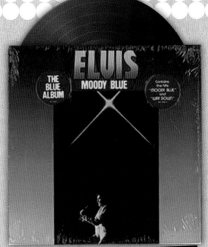

As Elvis left the building, this LP soundtracked his exit.

LEFT Elvis' physical and professional decline was plain to see.

ABOVE CBS aired a special live recording after Elvis died.

RIGHT The news nobody wanted, but probably expected, sadly.

Moody Blue is actually far less moody than its predecessor, *From Elvis Presley Boulevard, Memphis, Tennessee*—but its title suddenly became irrelevant when, four weeks after its release, Elvis died and his fans scrambled to buy his latest product. Be advised that "product" is the operative word here: like so many of Elvis' late-career albums, it feels as if zero effort was put into it by RCA or anyone else, making it just one more Elvis conveyor-belt item.

Still, there are one or two decent songs amid the processed slush. Half live, half recorded at Graceland, *Moody Blue* gives us a great title track, written by Mark "Suspicious Minds" James. This song had been a hit single on the country charts in early 1977, and with good reason. In similar vein, Elvis delivered a competent interpretation of George Jones's "She Thinks I Still Care."

There's a touch of variety on the LP, given the disco-flavored "Way Down," but by and large he sticks to the tried-and-true area of country and pop. He does attempt a rock 'n' roll homage with the previously unreleased "Little Darlin'." The track written by Tim Rice and Andrew Lloyd Webber, "It's Easy For You," has some spirited moments, as does Elvis' version of "Pledging My Love," but the album is let down by boring live songs such as "Let Me Be There."

TRACKLIST

SIDE ONE

1 Unchained Melody
2 If You Love Me (Let Me Know)
3 Little Darlin'
4 He'll Have to Go
5 Let Me Be There

SIDE TWO

1 Way Down
2 Pledging My Love
3 Moody Blue
4 She Thinks I Still Care
5 It's Easy for You

Images Elvis Presley (album covers), Getty Images, Alamy

CHAPTER 4
FALL of a King

Elvis
has LEFT
the BUILDING

Could the early death of Elvis Presley have been prevented? We explore the sad road to his demise at the age of only 42.

TOP Elvis in 1977—swollen and sweaty.

MIDDLE Colonel Tom is often seen as the villain who drove Elvis into the ground.

RIGHT Linda Thompson, girlfriend of Elvis for four years, with Dr. Nichopoulos.

The story of the decline and death of Elvis Presley is one from which we can all learn. He passed away at the age of 42, a devastating fact in its own right—even before we consider the sequence of events that led to his death. Officially, Elvis succumbed to cardiac arrhythmia, but this is disputed—in today's more health-conscious era, most of us understand the consequences of a deadly combination of depression, drug addiction, an exhausting lifestyle, and a destructive diet.

What's shocking is that it all happened so fast. Like many of us, Elvis gained and lost weight regularly during his adult life, but he was in relatively good shape as late as 1973, just four years before his death. However, behind the scenes he was dealing with addictions to barbiturates and pethidine, ordered for him by his physician, Dr. George C. Nichopoulos. Both of these substances hospitalized him that year. His use of these drugs was exacerbated by the emotional freefall he experienced after his divorce from Priscilla that October, and although he tried to give them up on several occasions, this was just too difficult for him.

In this, we should be sympathetic rather than judgmental. Have you ever tried to quit something relatively innocuous such as caffeine or nicotine? Then you'll know how hard it is. Now imagine quitting a powerful opiate that sustains you through an exhausting daily ritual, that is your only source of rest, and without which you will suffer dreadful withdrawal symptoms. Food seems to have been an addiction, too—raised to love high-fat recipes in an environment and at a time when nutrition was poorly understood, Elvis always regarded food both as comfort and security.

If Elvis had been allowed to take a couple of years off from touring, he might have had the opportunity and the motivation

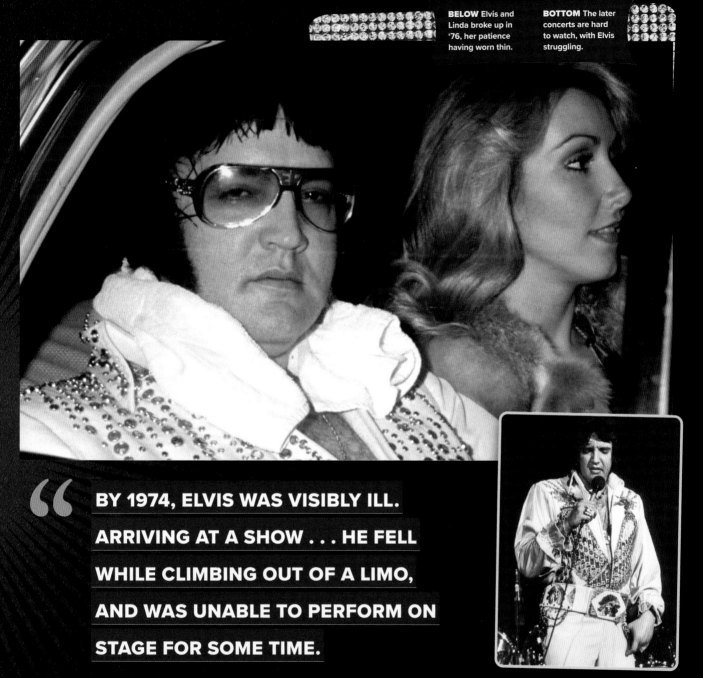

> **BY 1974, ELVIS WAS VISIBLY ILL. ARRIVING AT A SHOW . . . HE FELL WHILE CLIMBING OUT OF A LIMO, AND WAS UNABLE TO PERFORM ON STAGE FOR SOME TIME.**

to clean up, get fit, and emerge happier and healthier. In fact, he did the polar opposite as his health failed, performing an exhausting 168 shows in 1973, his busiest year ever. That would have been a challenging workload even for a physically fit musician half Elvis' age.

So why didn't he take time out? It's easy to blame Colonel Tom, whose own gambling addiction kept him in need of money from his cash-cow client, and who never showed much sympathy for Elvis' plight. That conclusion would be a little

too simple, however, and in fact a couple of other factors come into play here—not least the astounding fact that Elvis' extravagant lifestyle meant that he actually needed to work.

While the millions continued to roll in, just as much flew out again thanks to Elvis' habit of buying Cadillacs for his buddies in the Memphis Mafia, running a private jet, and supporting Graceland. There is no evidence to suggest that Elvis' huge wealth was actually about to run out, but there is said to have been tangible concern that one

day, it just might. With a background as poverty-stricken as his, it's understandable that he would do anything rather than suffer that fate.

By 1974, Elvis was visibly ill. Arriving at a show at the University of Maryland, he fell while climbing out of a limo, and was unable to perform on stage for some time, holding on to his microphone stand for support. His band was shocked to see him in this condition, with bassist Norbert Putnam telling *Bass Player* magazine many years

ABOVE Elvis' casket leaves Graceland, past streets of fans.

TOP RIGHT Ginger Alden, the last person to see Elvis alive.

RIGHT Mourners gathered outside Graceland the day after Elvis died.

later, "I asked our producer Felton Jarvis about Elvis' health, and he said, 'Well, he just gained so much weight. Last week I saw him eat a dozen eggs and a pound of bacon for breakfast.' I said, 'You're kidding?' and he said, 'The day before that, he binged on banana splits—he had a dozen of them.'"

Putnam continued, "'Is it just obesity that's the problem?' because I thought that could be dealt with, but Felton said, 'No, it's more than that. Elvis has been pretty depressed lately.' I said, 'Can't the Colonel do something?' and he told me that Elvis had been in the hospital several times to get off his medication, but it just hadn't worked."

Despite all this, Elvis continued to make music. A December 1973 session produced two albums' worth of songs, and in 1974 he released *Elvis Recorded Live on Stage in Memphis*, winning a Grammy for "How Great Thou Art." In 1976, RCA sent a mobile recording unit to Graceland for two sessions, with mixed results.

From 1972 to '76, Elvis had enjoyed the companionship of Linda Thompson, undoubtedly his most important romantic partner after Priscilla—but as time passed, her patience became understandably exhausted and the couple split in November

that year. By then, Elvis was a shadow of his former self, with his face swollen and pale and his voice weakened. Priscilla recalled that she met him around this time and was profoundly shocked at his appearance. Nonetheless, he did connect with a new girlfriend, Ginger Alden, to whom he even proposed, although few of his inner circle took this seriously.

By this time, Elvis' concerts were short—often less than an hour—and his spoken and singing voice hard to understand. He spent most of his time in bed, reading spiritualist books, watching TV, or lying in a drug-assisted trance. A real blow came in 1976 when Vernon Presley fired Red West and two other members of the Memphis Mafia, Sonny West and Dave Hebler, who promptly retaliated by writing a tell-all book called *Elvis: What Happened?*. Elvis tried and failed to block its publication, and its allegations of drug use shocked the world. When it came out on August 1, 1977, it devastated him.

Fifteen days after the book came out, Elvis was found dead in his private bathroom by Ginger Alden. He had suffered what appeared to be a fatal heart attack while on the toilet, and had fallen to the floor in a frozen, seated position. Emergency services could not revive him, and he was pronounced dead at Baptist Memorial Hospital in Memphis in the afternoon of August 16.

Once Colonel Tom—who snickered, "Why, I'll keep right on managing him!"—had informed the press that Elvis had died, a huge publicity event swung into action, with thousands of fans gathering at Graceland to view Elvis in his casket. One of his cousins, Billy Mann, was paid $18,000 to photograph the body, and the image appeared on the cover of the National Enquirer. Alden also signed a one hundred thousand dollar deal with the same "newspaper" for her story.

President Jimmy Carter stated that Elvis had "permanently changed the face

ABOVE Over 10,000 mourning fans tried to push into Graceland.

LEFT Elvis' casket being carried into the mausoleum.

BOTTOM LEFT Fans mourn Elvis at his funeral on August 8, 1977.

REST IN PEACE ELVIS

> " HE SPENT MOST OF HIS TIME IN BED, READING SPIRITUALIST BOOKS, WATCHING TV, OR LYING IN A DRUG-ASSISTED TRANCE.

of American popular culture," but sadly it turned out that Elvis received more attention that summer than he had in years. His funeral and interment took place at Graceland on August 18 and, as we'll go on to see, actually marked the beginning of a commercial golden age for the Elvis brand.

All that remained was for Elvis' fans to understand the manner of his passing, but sadly, this has never really been clarified. Toxicology reports revealed that 14 drugs were found in Elvis' system, although the local medical examiner, Jerry Francisco, stated that they played no role in his death; the autopsy also indicated that anaphylactic shock might have played a part, while a 1979 review concluded that a combination of central nervous system depressants had been the cause. As late as 1994, a Miami-Dade County coroner stated, "Everything points to a sudden, violent heart attack."

Perhaps the bigger picture is that life was just too much to handle for Elvis. In terms of health, he was dealt a bad genetic hand at birth—remember, his mother Gladys died at only 46. That, plus the drugs, the food, the depression, and the exhaustion did the trick. It was being Elvis that killed Elvis.

LONG

Elvis lives on, culturally and commercially, like no other musician before or since.

E lvis Presley lived for 42 years and has been dead for more than 45, and yet he's as well known in death as he was in life. Why is this?

Well, let's consider the data for a moment. He scored six Top 10 hits in the USA between his death in 1977 and 1981, the year before Graceland—which now brings in over 500,000 visitors a year, the most-visited home in the USA after the White House—opened to the public. In the decade after his death, he was given in absentia the Blues Foundation's WC Handy Award, the Academy of Country Music's Golden Hat Award, and the American Music Awards' Award of Merit. Elvis was also inducted into the Rock and Roll Hall of Fame, the Country Music Hall of Fame, the Gospel Music Hall of Fame, the Rockabilly Hall of Fame, and the Memphis Music Hall of Fame between the years 1986 and 2012.

Did the accolades—and associated income—stop there? Of course not. Colonel Tom ran the Presley brand until 1983, when legal investigations into his business practices saw him kicked out. He lived on until 1997, and at his funeral, Priscilla drily pointed out that she expected to have to pay for a ticket to leave the event. However, much as the Colonel can be criticized for bleeding Elvis dry and throwing him to the wolves, the most profitable exploitation

LEFT A statue of Elvis on his beloved Beale Street, Memphis, TN.

RIGHT Colonel Tom had an "interesting" approach to managing Elvis.

LIVE *The* KING

of Elvis has taken place since his death—at the hands of Elvis Presley Enterprises, the entity that handles his posthumous business. Colonel Tom himself remarked, "I don't think I exploited Elvis as much as he's being exploited today."

The appalling old shark had a point here. Elvis, in the hands of EPE, pioneered the idea of huge posthumous earnings. The implication here

is not that this was a bad thing: far from it. If Elvis' name, face, and music can be kept in the commercial bloodstream, then that can only be good for a new generation of fans. Older hands might sneer at the idea, but when Elvis appeared in hologram form in 2007 on *American Idol*—where he "performed" a song with Celine Dion—it was convincing enough to silence the most vocal critics. A full hologram tour has yet to happen more than 15 years later, but when—not if—it does, it will be worth seeing for anyone with even a passing interest in Elvis.

And why stick to the old songs? In 2012 Elvis scored a massive international hit with a big-beat remix of his song "A Little Less Conversation" from a DJ called Junkie XL, whose stage name could perhaps have been reconsidered considering the health problems that Elvis suffered in life. Used in a Nike advertising campaign during the 2002 World Cup, this song was number one in over 20 countries. Another remix, "Rubberneckin'," was a widespread hit the following year.

A long sequence of reissues of Elvis' chart-topping hits followed in 2005, along with a box set, helping to bring in vast sums of posthumous cash: for the next five years, *Forbes* magazine ranked him among its highest-earning dead artists, making between $45 million and $60 million per annum. There are huge, living bands who make a fraction of that sum, but then they don't have 15,000 licensed products with their names on them to sell, and they also don't own an entertainment complex called Elvis Presley's Memphis, or a hotel called The Guest House at Graceland.

So much for the numbers. Let's see how Elvis engendered real, cultural change that is nothing to do with massive piles of cash.

Rightly or wrongly, Elvis brought Black music to a White audience, legitimizing music

ABOVE Little Richard is just one act who influenced a young Elvis.

LEFT Graceland continues to draw crowds, especially on major dates.

BELOW Could Elvis have understood the breadth of his influence?

"ELVIS WAS A BLESSING. THEY WOULDN'T LET BLACK MUSIC THROUGH. HE OPENED THE DOOR FOR BLACK MUSIC."

★ *Little Richard*

of African-American origin for a demographic who would otherwise have avoided it. Yes, he made millions, which a Black performer of equivalent style would not have done. Yes, he essentially appropriated African-American culture—this is understood. One positive consequence of this was that Black musicians enjoyed commercial acceptance for the first time. Through Elvis, rock 'n' roll pioneered by Little Richard and Chuck Berry, not to mention the hundreds of African-American

jazz, swing, blues, and gospel musicians who fueled the rock 'n' roll sound, found a home in the American psyche, and from there around the world.

As Little Richard said, "He was an integrator. Elvis was a blessing. They wouldn't let Black music through. He opened the door for Black music." The soul singer Al Green added: "He broke the ice for all of us." Jackie Wilson stated: "A lot of people have accused Elvis of stealing the Black man's music, when in fact, almost

every Black solo entertainer copied his stage mannerisms from Elvis."

A consequence of Elvis' early stage performances was that a new archetype was born: the sexually charged singer with a guitar. Elvis played, sang, and swayed his hips at the same time, and while he was no virtuoso on any instrument, guitar-slingers from The Beatles to Eddie Van Halen to George Ezra and beyond owe him a visual debt, whether they know it or not. Even the conductor Leonard Bernstein once opined, "Elvis Presley is the greatest cultural force in the 20th century. He introduced the beat to everything, and he changed everything—music, language, clothes. It's a whole new social revolution—the sixties came from it."

Then there's the idea of the American Dream: the concept that any member of the American public can rise from poverty and make themselves rich, or at least survive, through a solid work ethic and the acquisition of capital. No one epitomizes this trajectory better than Elvis, although in his particular case, his journey from literal rags to riches should come with a health warning—if you make a lot of money, don't let it kill you. That aside, his story is perfectly tailored to the popular postwar fantasy of the fifties to the seventies, with the silly trappings of wealth—Cadillacs, Las Vegas, Hollywood—as much the focus as the actual contents of Elvis' bank account.

Is Elvis even dead? Thousands of slightly irrational fans apparently think not, with "sightings" frequently reported. After all, had Elvis faked his own death, perhaps by paying off his family and household and escaping to Mexico, he could still be alive today. Two documentaries, *The Elvis Files* (1991) and *The Elvis Conspiracy* (1992) explore this idea, and of course you can go to Las Vegas and be entertained, and even legally married, by an Elvis impersonator. Tribute singers to Elvis abound worldwide, of varying levels of quality.

As the decades pass, our prediction is that the Elvis industry will only continue to expand. Graceland, the heartland of his brand, remains hugely popular. Every year on August 16, a procession of fans wends its way past Elvis' grave, with 40,000 mourners doing so on the 25th anniversary in 2002. In doing this, they pay tribute to the life and work of a unique musician—a flawed genius whose light remains undimmed, all these years later.

You may ask the question "Why did Elvis die so young?" Perhaps the answer is that he didn't really die, other than in a strictly physical sense. After all, he's still with us in so many ways. Can the same be said of any other departed musician?

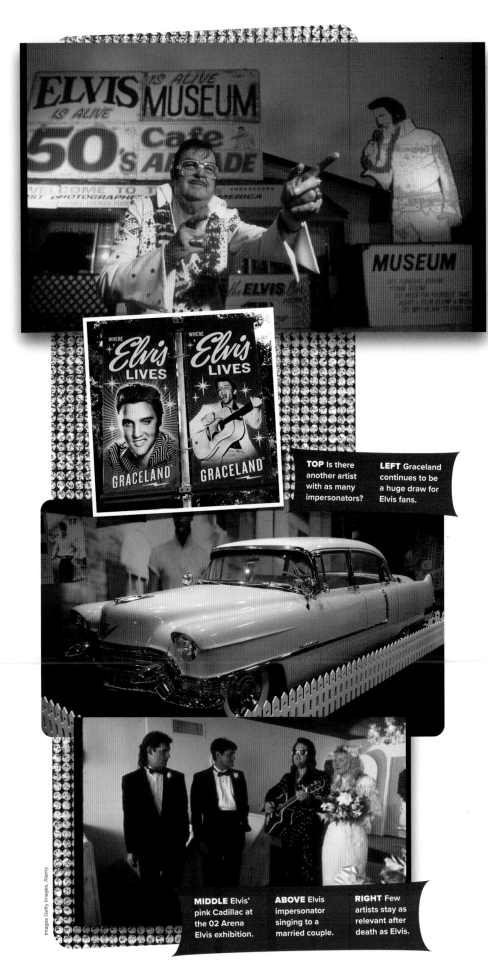

TOP Is there another artist with as many impersonators?

LEFT Graceland continues to be a huge draw for Elvis fans.

MIDDLE Elvis' pink Cadillac at the 02 Arena Elvis exhibition.

ABOVE Elvis impersonator singing to a married couple.

RIGHT Few artists stay as relevant after death as Elvis.

Images Getty Images, Alamy

"WHILE HE WAS NO VIRTUOSO ON ANY INSTRUMENT, GUITAR-SLINGERS FROM THE BEATLES TO GEORGE EZRA OWE HIM A VISUAL DEBT.

Thank you,
thank you very much.